RIDING THE INTUITIVE WAVE

Learn To Listen To What Your Body Already Knows

RIDING THE INTUITIVE WAVE

Linda Eastburn

Endue Publishing
Springfield, Missouri

For Information Write:

Endue Publishing
Springfield, Missouri
 call: 417-863-1377

ISBN:0-9778830-0-0

Library of Congress Catalog Card Number Pending:

Printed in the United States of America
By: Litho Printers & Bindery
     Cassville, MO

Table of Contents

INTRODUCTION

The mysteries of life both confuse and haunt my curious mind. There is so much that can not be explained and yet I am always in pursuit of trying. This is especially true regarding human consciousness.

Self-understanding is something I have sought for many years, yet I don't know why I prefer the color green over brown, why I am so drawn to scientific research, nor why my life has been so greatly blessed while others struggle with adversity. I do know some things, however. I know I am able to expand my consciousness, go past what current science says is possible, and be aware of things outside my physical perception. In other words, I can see things on the other side of the world, know someone's thoughts, and even witness the future.

I have not always been intuitive. I spent forty years in conscious confinement. Like most people, I believed I existed on an isle of solitude where my thoughts were hidden, my desires secret, and perception limited to my five senses. I now know different. I know, not because I watched someone else do it or because I read it in a book, but because I experience these things daily.

I am a professional intuitive which means I work in a field of expanded consciousness. I see inside the human body to find diseases, look at thoughts and emotions to help people find personal clarity, locate missing people, look at crime scenes, and go into the future to see the outcome of events.

Unlike most people who work in this field, I was not born naturally intuitive. Only after years of self-discipline and training did I become skilled. I learned how to expand my consciousness, direct my focus, and access a great reservoir of information despite the fact I was born intuitively challenged. I have not, as of yet, found any subject, time period, or solution to a problem absent from discovery in this sea of wisdom I call universal mind. It contains accounts of everything, no matter how small and fleeting, or how vast and life changing.

Through the pages of this book, I will share many of my intuitive experiences, show how I learned to be intuitive, and give you the means to do the same. Through my years of teaching, I have found ways to swiftly help you learn, apply the skill to daily life, and even use intuition to manifest your desires. It is a natural and normal part of your consciousness so enjoy your expansive journey.

Chapter One

WHAT THE EYE CAN NOT YET SEE

ANN

By midnight my concern for Ann outweighed any obstacle of finding her. As soon as I found out she had left home and no one knew her whereabouts, I was instantly worried. The thought of her needing help haunted me until I finally got in my car to search for her.

In a city with hundreds of apartment buildings, finding her would be difficult. Even so I knew I had to try. Pulling out of my driveway, I sensed the direction I should go. I anticipated each turn until ending up on a street with rows of apartment buildings on each side. As soon as I felt the urge, I pulled into one. I circled the parking lot with little hope not expecting to find her. I then looked up to see someone standing on a second story balcony. I recognized her immediately, even though her face was shadowed by the darkness of the night. It was Ann.

Like some kind of unexplained radar, I was guided directly to her presence. Only a few moments before, I hadn't a clue how to find her. Now she stood alone, looking out over the cold unfamiliar night, just as I looked up to see her unmoving dark silhouette standing in the glass doorway. The well lit room

3

behind her showed no sign that anyone actually lived there. It was as empty as I imagined her heart must be feeling. I wanted to speak with her so I pulled around to the entrance of the building. I had no idea what I would say as I climbed the stairs and walked down the hall. While knocking on the door, I mustered up a few cheery lines, explaining why I would possibly be there at this time of night.

There was a long wait before a thin wiry man opened the door partway. He glared at me with suspicion. I smiled and tried to look as much at ease as I could before asking for Ann. Saying her name made him even more leery of my motives, and he immediately denied knowing her.

I felt certain I was at the right door, so I explained I was a relative and really needed to see her. Before finishing the sentence, I heard her voice and then saw her as she opened the door a little wider. Obviously, she was surprised to see me since no one knew where she was living. Now she was staring at me with a puzzled look, no doubt wondering why I was there.

I felt awkward standing at her door but it wasn't the first time I had ended up in a strange situation. I chose my words carefully not wanting to seem judgmental or take anyone's side. My intent was only to be a support for her and a doorway back into her life if she wanted one. We talked casually for a while, and then I left making certain she had my number if she needed anything at all.

Only a few days later, she called wanting to talk. She felt she had made a big mistake and now wanted to return home. There were some family issues, but I assured her these were minor things that could be overcome. I drove her home and watched as she walked back into her life.

EIGHT THOUSAND DOLLAR MIRACLE

Jacquelyn Aldana, author of *The 15-Minute Miracle,* is a good friend of mine. She has one of the most inspiring stories I have ever heard that led her to the process described in her book. She often refers clients to me or calls when she needs some intuitive information.

One day I received a call from her. She was desperately looking for eight thousand misplaced dollars. Her husband had sold a car the evening before and was paid in cash for the automobile. He walked in the house with the money, and rather than placing it where he normally would, he put it in a small box on the desk in the office.

Later Jacquelyn and her husband Ron went out for dinner. The next morning Jacquelyn, having no idea there was eight thousand dollars in the box, picked it up and placed it on the wooden file cabinet. When Ron began to look for the money, he couldn't find it. With no memory of placing it in the box the evening before, he looked in the money bag where it should have been. The money was not there. After searching the room, he called for Jacquelyn to help.

They looked in several obvious places before Jacquelyn finally called me and explained the situation. She asked if I could take a look, even though I was in Missouri and the money was in California. I started by commenting how it was not in the red money bag where it normally would have been. This alone was enough to convince her I was intuitively there since I had no way of knowing they even owned a red money bag.

I could tell the money was in a box. It looked to be some sort of container that was molded like plastic. The next thing I saw was light colored wood. I could feel the texture and see the color like a light oak or pine. The money seemed to be at a height of about five or six feet above the floor.

Jacquelyn relayed the information to her husband. He looked around the room for anything that fit the description. He identified the box I had described. He opened the lid, looked inside, and there was the money.

SEEING A CHILD'S LIFE BEFORE BIRTH

Evelyn sat in the chair across from me. She had finished asking all the questions about herself so to end the session she asked about her unborn grandchild. The birth date was in a few months and she was eager for information.

I intuitively looked at the unborn child's future. I could see he would be a very hyper child with strong sensitivities, seeing angels, and being naturally intuitive. I looked at his family's response to this and they seemed troubled by his abilities. I then saw something I was very reluctant to share with his grandmother. He was going to have a severe disease during his childhood, but he would fully recover. Because it seemed like a major event in his life, I went ahead and told her. Over all, I described him as a high maintenance child that needed special care and attention.

Four years went by after this session. There was a group of people gathered in my living room including a young woman whom I had never met before. She started talking about her four year old son. She was troubled by his ability to see the future, speak with angels, and his often hyper state of mind.

The woman went on to talk about her son having survived cancer. In his short life he had been a handful. Then she looked at me and said it was just as I had seen before he was born, he was a high maintenance child. Her son was Evelyn's grandchild that I had looked at in the womb four years before.

6

AN INTUITIVE LOOK AT THE BODY

Joe was an old friend of mine but I had not seen him for years. This day I received a message on my machine simply stating he was in the hospital. I tried contacting his wife with no luck, so I called the hospital where I discovered he was in intensive care. They wouldn't give any further information but I realized it was serious.

I debated what to do. I felt paralyzed but wanted to help in any way possible. My ability to intuitively see his condition was the one thing I could do, but under the circumstance, could not ask his permission. The ethical question haunted me for a few moments as I decided the best course of action. I determined to ask his mind directly. His voice came back in a silent echo. "Help me. Help me. Help me."

Joe was slipping into a coma as I sat down to do the session. His lifeless body lay still in the sterile hospital bed as his organs began to fail one by one. The test results gave his physicians no direction for diagnosis or treatment. They could only monitor his condition and try to keep him alive.

I placed the tape in the recorder as I had done a thousand times before. Closing my eyes, I began to go into a deep trance state. I connected with Joe and focused on his condition. A sadness came over me as I could see how severe it was. I saw his kidneys shutting down. His pancreas and kidneys were at war in his body trying to steal every drop of life force to stay functioning.

His body was extremely toxic from what seemed to be some sort of virus. This caused a great deal of mucus to form in the body a few weeks earlier, prohibiting the lungs and lymphatic system from doing their job. On top of this, he had inhaled something which created an even stronger toxic condition for the

7

body to deal with. Toxic fluids now permeated the body causing the organs some major difficulty. There wasn't enough oxygen to sustain him. His whole system looked to be shutting down as I finished the session.

I could see his best hope was a major detoxification, not something he was likely to get in the hospital. I didn't know what he was going through emotionally at the time, but I could tell he was in great conflict. This conflict had contributed to the war between his pancreas and kidneys. Neither had much life left in them.

He had temporally escaped the harsh reality of his life as he debated with his fate. The decision to live or die was not yet determined, but his soul was asking for aid. My heart reached out to him in response to his request.

This conflict had been years in coming, and now he was forced to face this emotional issue. I had no idea what was going on in his personal life and didn't feel it was any of my business. I only knew how he was responding to it and that was hard.

I opened my eyes and felt the tears running down my cheeks. I was always so objective in these sessions but this time I couldn't stop crying. Joe was my friend and he was in serious trouble.

I walked out of the house with the tape and headed to the hospital. I only hoped his wife would be there when I arrived. I walked through the corridors to the intensive care unit and into the waiting room. His wife, Teresa, looked up just as I entered. We embraced one another with an intensity that confirmed I was correct in my knowledge of Joe's condition. I handed her the tape and told her to do whatever she wished with the information.

She wanted to talk and I was very emotionally available

to listen. She shared that Joe had contracted what he thought was the flu a few days prior to being admitted to the hospital. He had just returned home from a family reunion when he began to feel ill. His brother found him in a very bad state and rushed him to the emergency room just two days ago. They had not been able to locate the cause of his illness. He had slipped into a coma just a few hours before I arrived.

She opened up to me and shared the personal side of their story. She had told Joe only a few weeks before she wanted a divorce. I was saddened to hear this news, but understood their relationship had been very shaky for years. I then realized what Joe was facing. Teresa took me down the hall to see him. His weak body looked lifeless against the white sheets. Only the motionless shell of his being remained. This struggle was happening within him, and no one knew if he would return.

I drove home in prayer. Respecting his free will, I did not ask for intervention from outside sources to rescue his life. After all, who was I to determine if life or death would be best for him. I did plead and reason with him about the value of his life, however. I reminded him of the many who loved him. His self-judgment was far too harsh at this time. I projected images of a positive future for him to consider, reminding him of hope.

I received a call from Teresa early the next morning. They were moving Joe to another hospital in order to put him on dialysis. The session was right, his kidneys were shutting down the evening before.

Teresa had listened to the tape and then offered it to Joe's physician. We had no way of knowing if she listened, but shortly thereafter, they were running tests on many of the things mentioned in the tape. They did conclude it must be some sort of viral condition, but they had no idea how to treat it.

9

Meanwhile Joe remained in a coma. Days went by and he did not return to consciousness. They began to prepare his wife for the worst, telling her he might have brain damage even if he came out of the coma. They were going to run tests to see if he had suffered a stroke and to determine the supply of blood to the brain. His fever was peeking throughout the day, also causing some concern.

With this news I received a call from Teresa, now very upset. She had prepared herself for the possibility of his death; but nowhere had she allowed for the potential of his remaining alive and being a vegetable. She needed help dealing with this, and asked if I would look at his condition once again.

I entered an intuitive state again and looked closely at his brain and nervous system. I did not see any damage. It looked as though he would be out of the coma in a few days, but he would be very mentally groggy. He would not be fully conscious for two weeks when he would then begin to speak. He would fully recover and the body would return to a state of health, but it would take two years before he would enjoy the same physical condition he had before.

I took the session to Teresa. She was relieved to hear my words. They were obviously comforting to her after the projections being told her by the hospital. No one knew if what I saw would play out that way, but it allowed for hope in a dire situation.

Joe came out of the coma in a few days. I stopped by the hospital often to check his condition. His eyes were glazed over with a distant stare. Occasionally he would look in my direction, but there were no signs of recognition. Day after day I noticed more eye contact, but he was aware of my presence only part of the time. He slowly began to speak again which was a major relief to everyone. The hospital had stabilized his body enough that he had survived. Joe continued to improve over the next two years until he became a fully functioning, healthy person again.

I AM AN INTUITIVE

The stories above are real sessions, mostly from the archives of my work. As a professional intuitive, I have had the opportunity to work with a variety of subjects, but also use the skill daily in my personal life. Because I use my intuition regularly, there is no doubt it works, is very natural, and a very real part of my mental perception.

Anyone with normal intelligence is capable of learning intuition as well. In order to learn, you must be disciplined enough to practice however. Many take a weekend course and leave disappointed they are not at a prime performance level. What is often misunderstood is how a really good intuitive will acquire the skill by the same means as a good athlete or musician. It requires honing the skill through daily discipline.

I am a trained intuitive having had very minimal experience before I turned forty. It all began when I attended a metaphysical school back in 1989. The school had a very regimented program requiring several hours of exercises per day. The drop out rate was enormous because the program demanded so much of the student's time. I refer to this training as my boot camp of self-awareness, because it was so rigid.

Looking back, the school was the best place for me at that time. It no doubt accelerated my intuitive development, even though that wasn't why I attended. I was looking for self-awareness and discovered far more than I bargained for. The program began with dream analysis, and in a year and a half, I was having profound visions through a deep meditation called Hong Sau. The exercises gave me the focus, concentration, and sensitivity, required to be intuitive.

The funny thing is while I was at the school, I wasn't intuitive at all. Every week we did an intuitive exercise in class which involved twenty five color cards. Each card had a circle with one of five colors. Our teacher would shuffle the cards and one by one mentally project the color of the card she was holding. Chance said we should get 5 out of twenty five by just guessing. Anything over 5 was above average. Some students got twenty one to twenty five correct every week but that wasn't me. I only got seven to nine cards correct each time we played. I was really not intuitive at that time.

I learned a great deal about myself, but I didn't learn intuition directly from this school. What the program did do for me was prime my mind. I learned how to meditate, and even established a two-way dialog with my inner self, by practicing expectant listening. I could ask a question for guidance through my meditation and receive an answer in return. I wasn't intuitive when I left the school in 1991, but I was soon after.

I continued to do the mental exercises while attending an internship in hypnosis. This was a major complement to the metaphysical course I had completed. The four months of daily attendance, observing the practice of a veteran hypnotist, only added to the knowledge I already had. I learned how to go into a deep trance state and hold my attention there for hours.

It isn't really one class I can say taught me to be intuitive. It is the combination of mental concentration, meditation, and hypnosis to which I contribute my intuitive development. Without applying myself to each of these, my intuition would not have grown as strong.

I now teach intuition and have added many exercises of my own to help you learn the skill. Since I was trained, I observed what was needed, making it easier to transfer this knowledge to others. Things like sensitivity, receptivity, and shifting the brain and heart frequencies for better intuitive reception, are included.

Chapter Two

BEFORE INTUITION

CHILDHOOD

It was against all odds I ended up intuitive. I grew up in a rural community in Missouri, the baby of an extended family, consisting of my parents, sister, uncle and grandmother. We lived on a small farm, and had a very normal life attending church on Sunday, growing our own food, and having family gatherings.

My childhood memories mostly consist of playing out of doors in our big shaded yard up to the time I was six. Our dog, Corkie, a mix between a chow and collie, was a friendly companion. He was like a big furry bear, and took on the role of my protector when I was young.

The yard was a world to explore with dangers as well as pleasant surprises. There were areas to avoid, like the tall oak trees along the far edge of the yard, where snakes hung from the branches. I once discovered a tiny stream in the ditch along the driveway after a rain. I ran into the house, and asked my mother to make butter and sorghum sandwiches, so I could have a picnic while watching the miniature waterfall over the rocks.

When I was six, we built a new house and moved. My familiar shaded play area was replaced by a sunny barren yard.

The only salvation of this new home was the year round stream running through the pasture. I explored the land for hours at a time, staying away from the house, returning only for meals. The acreage transformed into the entire world through my imagination. Switzerland was on the hillside covered with persimmon trees. The sand dunes, on the back side of the property caused by the wind, became Israel. And the small stream was covered in pirates, sailing ships, and Huck Finn's raft, depending on my mood.

No one in my family was intuitive, even though my mother was very perceptive, making it difficult to get away with anything. Our spiritual life conformed to the community, rooted in a conservative Baptist faith. I was very drawn to the beliefs of our church, and took all the teachings very seriously. As a teen, I didn't want to miss services on Sunday, and was one of the few who enjoyed Wednesday night bible study. The congregation, mostly the elderly men of the church, gathered to learn more about the word of God. I found their wisdom to be very stimulating and far more enjoyable than the Sunday School of my peers. Even though I wasn't intuitive, I did have two prophetic dreams prior to developing my intuition. Both were at important moments of my life, impacted me emotionally, and revealed some very significant events that were about to unfold. The first involved a very frightening situation. It was a person I knew well and trusted. In the dream, this individual grew out of control and their eyes looked very disturbed. Within a few weeks, I witnessed this event right before my eyes.

EARLY ADULTHOOD

After graduating from high school, I had several odd jobs while taking some college courses. I never graduated because I couldn't decide on a major. I liked art but was also drawn to psychology. Later, I took a real interest in business, and regretted not pursuing a degree more diligently. What I really wanted to do was real estate investing. Unfortunately, it required far more cash than I had at the time.

My interest in real estate started when I was a teenager after Mr. Nimo moved in next door to my parents. He was a retired high school principal who spent his summers fixing up houses. He accumulated quite a bit of wealth from this, which he was more than happy to talk about.

Mr. Nimo inspired my interest in real estate, but it was a handsome young man from whom I purchased my first automobile, that peaked my interest further. His goal was to own apartment buildings as his father did. He convinced me it was a great investment and quite lucrative, adding to the vision already established in my mind by Mr. Nimo. I had a ways to go before that day would come, but I never lost sight of the goal.

In my early twenties, I started working for a wholesale western goods business. Bert, the owner, was a wheeler dealer type with a huge ego. A self-made man, starting his business with nothing more than a dream, he managed to carve out a nice little niche in the market. I was young and had no experience in wholesale. I started out doing clerical work and a little production. My job description progressed with time, and I ended up managing the operation. It was a good experience for me and obviously Bert saw something in me I didn't.

While working for Bert, I started a relationship that lasted seven years ending in a year and a half marriage. Before the demise of this union, I had my second prophetic dream. This time I saw the face of a woman I did not know but felt was a threat to me. She was very attractive with long brunette hair falling past her waist and big dark eyes. She was close enough I could see her features clearly. She only looked at me, yet it disturbed me to such a degree, I began to question why.

When I saw the woman for the first time, I knew she was the one in my dream. An odd feeling came over my body as I tried to reason why I was feeling so ill. Within a few weeks, I found out my husband had been having an affair with her for most of our short marriage. Once again I had been warned through a dream of an emotional event in advance.

Outside of the two dreams, I had only a few glimpses of my intuition. Mostly they were around the time of my divorce at the age of twenty seven. During this marriage, I started having dreams about my house burning down. After a few nights of this, I turned on the television one day to find a scene of a fire. It felt a little eerie because it reminded me so much of the dreams I had been having. That same night, at two in the morning, the phone rang. Half asleep, I answered it to hear a woman screaming in my ear, that my house was on fire. I jumped up and ran outside looking for smoke and flames, when I realized it was a prank call.

This was all so puzzling to me because I couldn't put my finger on what was happening. Being both observant and curious, my mind wondered why. At the time, I could only make note of these strange synchronicities and let them go.

After my divorce, I had to reevaluate what I wanted from my life. It was a difficult emotional time for me and I prayed often, mostly for comfort. To my surprise, during one of my prayers, an answer came back. It wasn't an audible answer but a silent voice that I heard. It was simple and direct saying, "Linda, if you want your life to be different you simply must take responsibility for it." At the time, I felt this was a spiritual message, if not God himself, answering my prayer. The words spoke volumes to me, at the time, and have been a major inspiration ever since.

It was near this same time I began to recognize the power

of thought and how much it influences life. I started defining the type of relationship I really wanted, offering this as a kind of inner prayer. My list consisted of some important characteristics I wanted in a partner. They included things like honesty, integrity, and a person who really loved me. Within two weeks, a person came into my life possessing all I had asked for.

I married that person and something I call the golden years began. For the next ten years most everything we did turned out prosperous. We were on a creative binge. I observed several things that contributed to this good fortune. Our thinking was very positive, appreciative, and clear. We were in resonance with one another wanting to make our life work. It was as though I had discovered the pot of gold at the end of the rainbow, and it was all wrapped up in a loving package.

The subtleness of intuition continued to speak through lightly felt impressions. One lazy Sunday afternoon, I was scanning through a magazine, when I ran across a short psychological quiz. One question asked if it was possible to influence another person with thought alone. My first response was no, but then I stopped. Something prohibited me from writing down my answer. I knew if I circled the yes answer it would lower my score but I simply had to. I didn't know why this feeling was so strong, but I knew it was the truth.

I was in my early thirties when I finally realized my dream as a real estate investor. I attended real estate school, became a licensed agent, and bought my first rental house a few months later. It was a small home, with a dirt floored one car garage, that rented for the meager price of one hundred seventy-five dollars a month. It wasn't much of a house, but it was a place to start.

We didn't pay much for the house, but being novice investors, we still payed too much. When we wanted to sell the house after a few years, we couldn't get the price we wanted. Since the house had long paid for itself, we accepted an offer that was actually less than we had originally paid for it. In those days, we could insure the house for replacement value, which was several thousand more than the offer we had in hand.

While waiting for the closing papers to be prepared on the sale of the house, my sister came by one morning for coffee. We were all sitting at the kitchen table, talking about the house, when I made a comment about how the best thing that could happen to that house was if it burned down, not thinking my words would have any bearing whatsoever on the fate of the property.

When I arrived home that afternoon, I picked up my messages from the answering machine. A serious male voice sounded over the machine, requesting we get in touch with him about our house at such and such address, because it had burned down. I couldn't believe my ears. We had just been talking about this house burning down that morning and now it had. This was an eye opener for me. I began to observe how life works, suspecting we not only influence people with our thoughts, but situations of life as well.

The next several years of my life was all about real estate. One by one we built up our inventory of properties, started our own brokerage, and began some major rehab projects. During this period, I had time to explore some other interests.

I was listening to my body, understanding my feelings were knowledgeable. I had always been sensitive to my physical system, but now I was listening to these sensations even more. I didn't know what to call them or how much to trust them, but I was listening. I saw an ad in a local newspaper that offered free dream interpretation lectures. Remembering my two prophetic dreams, I felt the inclination to attend one.

I was thirty-six when I entered the doors of the metaphysical school for the first time. It was a tall, three story house with a huge porch stretching across the front. I rang the bell and a heavyset young woman answered the door and invited me in. I couldn't help but notice the tall dark wooden staircase in the foyer as I turned and entered the living room. A fireplace was at the far end of the room and a number of tall windows lined one wall. It was an old rambling house with antique furniture scattered about. I turned and entered the dining room where the lecture was to be held. It was crowded with an oversized antique table and matching buffet. This room also housed the bookstore, and held two walls full of books, floor to ceiling.

The woman began the lecture on dreams. Knowing nothing about the subject, I silently listened. She explained how our subconscious processes the experiences of our day and feeds them back in the form of dreams. Symbolic pictures are used. Everything in our dreams are a reflection of ourselves including people.

The interpretation process was easy to understand. People reflected aspects of ourselves, and things were interpreted based on their function. For instance, if I had a dream of a friend, all I need do is identify three outstanding characteristics of that person and then transfer those characteristics to myself. This shows what my dream is telling me about myself.

Things are interpreted by their function. A telephone is a means of communication, a chair a means of support, and a car a means of transportation or movement often representing the physical body. There are some exceptions to this process, but these are the basic rules.

After the lecture, I started keeping a dream journal. Each morning I wrote down my dreams and interpreted what I thought my subconscious mind was telling me. I learned a lot about myself, and after a few months, I felt certain I should attend the weekly classes offered by the school.

I enrolled and we started with simple meditation, along with a mental focus exercise. I was engrossed in self-discovery at that time, and found these people fascinating, with highly developed intuitive abilities. They could have whole conversations with one another and never speak a word. I was intrigued by what they knew, even though it was very different from anything I had been introduced to before.

Chapter Three

LEARNING TO SEE

DEVELOPING MY INTUITIVE SKILLS

Terri was the director of the school of metaphysics. She was one of many volunteers working for this institution, which taught the application of metaphysics in day to day life. Joining this school was the beginning of my intuitive development, even though I am not sure I would have started had I known just how rigorous it would become.

We began the course by learning meditation. It was a different sort of meditation than I had ever heard of before. Rather than stilling the mind, we were to ask a question and listen for an answer. This was to be done twenty minutes each morning, followed by writing in a dream journal, and then doing a mental focus exercise.

During this initial time at the school, my instructor encouraged our class to have an intuitive session. She explained how some leaders of the school had developed their intuition to such a degree as to be able to do what they called a reading. They offered a variety of these including life, life crossings, health, business, and family. I opted to do the health reading, knowing very little of what to expect.

Our class gathered early one evening, and caravanned to the headquarters of the school some sixty miles away. It was located on a self-supportive farm with cattle, barns, a chapel, and a large dorm facility. They not only did intuitive sessions, but also published several books, offered a college level program in metaphysics, and had regular Sunday services. Several people lived at the facility, where they made butter, cheese, and canned vegetables from their large garden.

We lined up in the living room as the people who lived there introduced themselves. There was a tall, thin woman wearing a long skirt and a pair of farm boots who had just come in from milking. There were a couple of middle-aged women smiling as they finished up the dinner dishes. I recognized a man with a long beard sitting at the dining table. He was a teacher from the school where I attended. A short, heavyset woman, much younger than the rest, came close to me. She reached out her hand to me but didn't let go. Her face was very close to me and for a moment, I thought she was actually trying to smell me. She stood there for what seemed like an eternity until finally walking away to my relief.

We all sat down in a semicircle around the living room, facing the couple who would conduct the intuitive sessions. Never having seen anything of this nature before, I was a little nervous. I was thankful there was one person ahead of me, which gave me the opportunity to observe a session before mine.

When it came my turn, I was asked to sit in a chair in front of the reader. The reader was a woman about my age with mid-length dark hair named Barbara. Her partner and hypnotic conductor, Dan, sat beside her. He seemed to be in charge. He directed her to go into a deep trance state where she stayed until all the sessions were over. As the people rotated, he gave her their names and the type of reading she was to do for them. As he gave her my name, I began to feel my pulse increase and my palms became moist. Not wanting to be embarrassed in front of this group, it was difficult to focus. He told her to examine all disorders, whether they be physical, emotional, or mental, and relate all things that might correct these disorders.

This is what she said. *"We see denial in the mental system. We see this particularly directed toward this one's own sense of understanding and this one's own intuitiveness. This one has had a tendency to downplay or ignore this part of the self, although it is very prevalent, and there is much attention that is drawn to it. This one does not accept a type of responsibility for it.*

In this way, this one does deny this one's own creative ability, and this one's own power in regard to this one's use of the mind. There is a need for this one to grow in respect for this one's capabilities, and for this one's skills, in being able to use more of this one's self than this one often agrees to live with or sees others as settling for. This one tends to compromise very easily. Each time this is done this one leads the self away from what is most desired. There is a need for this one to build a sense of strength of will, as well as a greater commitment to this one's own sense of well being, and this one's own growth and understanding. There are a variety of ways this one could hone this one's abilities and skills and many of these are known to this one.

In the emotional system, there is difficulty in this one being able to express the self fully, due to what has been given. Many times this one will tamper with and will restrict this one's emotional expression due to expected results from those in the environment. In this regard, this one allows the expectations of the self, in terms of what others will think, to rule this one's own expression rather than this one being creative and choosing the expression that this one might want to have at any given time. This one does have this capability of taking this type of control of

24

the emotions, however, this is not practiced because of what has been given.

As there is the respect built, and the willingness to commit the self to causing maturity and growth, there would be a recognition of emotional expression different from what this one has experienced.

Because of what has been given, there is a great deal of restriction in the physical body. There is difficulty in the skeletal system. This includes the skull plates as well as the vertebra. In addition to misalignments, there is difficulty in the balance of the spinal fluids and in the cerebral spinal fluid. There is difficulty particularly in regard to the back portion of the brain. This primarily is in regard to the workings of the nervous system in this area. This is sporadic and is in direct correlation with whether the skull is in alignment or not. Would suggest osteopathic or chiropractic attention in these areas. There is also a need for stimulation of the nerve trunks, particularly in the cervical region of the spinal column. There is some imbalance in the auditory system due to what has been given and there is some interference with the optical nerves as well. This would change as there would be some adjustment made.

There is tension in the endocrine system. This is particularly true with the interplay between the pituitary and the hypothalamus. There is a need for more trace minerals in this one's diet. There is also a need for relaxation and states of meditation to be experienced by this one, in order to cause there to be a stimulation of the hormonal production and release in the pituitary. There is some sluggishness in the thyroid and the adrenals. Would suggest the introduction of iodine in the diet would be of benefit. In the digestive system, there is a tendency toward sluggishness. Particularly in regards to the duodenal area and in moving into the small intestines. This body could benefit from ingestion of yogurt or buttermilk. There is a need for

25

stimulation of the liver. Citrus juices would be of benefit, particularly that of lemon. There is a tendency toward sluggishness in the circulatory system. There are times of low blood pressure experienced in this body. This is directly related to this one denying the understandings that have already been described. There is some difficulty in the lower portion of the spine. This is in regards to the third and fourth lumbar area. There is some compressing in this area, and there is a need for adjustment and stimulation of the nerve trunks, as well as stimulation of the muscles in this area. Gentle bending exercises would be of benefit to this body. Forms of hatha yoga could also be useful. This is all. "

Dan handed me the cassette, and I moved back to the chair behind me, thankful I had a tape. I related to what was said, but was also surprised that she saw me as intuitive.

I had no idea how she knew so much about me, but she had captured my life and my issues. I understood she saw an intuitive part of me I was denying. This reading, in part, was responsible for my intuitive development. I was curious to find out just how intuitive I really was. It served as a motivation and an inspiration.

THIS ISN'T FOR ME

After eight weeks of attending the school of metaphysics, I left. It was just too far from my spiritual roots. Even though I was no longer going to class, I continued doing the exercises. For three months, I awoke everyday and did the twenty minute meditation, asking a question and listening for an answer. I kept a journal of both my questions and answers during this time. I noticed the complexity and accuracy of my answers grow. As I continued to practice, the answers changed from a single word, to a few words, to a full sentence. After a time, I was having a full dialog in this meditative state.

I must admit I was very leery of this at first. I needed proof if this information was worthy of my attention. Day after day I would write down my meditation questions and answers. After several months of examining the answers, I began to trust it. It was solid, good practical advice.

MORE THAN MEETS THE EYE

The school not only introduced me to intuition, but it also introduced me to manifestation. Three months after attending my last class, my husband and I were planning a short weekend trip. It was a six hour drive from home. I wanted the weekend to be special, so I asked in meditation, how to make the trip most enjoyable.

The answer was simple and short. I was to let every thought I had be positive. This didn't sound too complicated. As a matter of fact, it sounded so simple, I doubted it was really much of an answer.

We started the trip early on Friday morning. A few hours into the trip, driving down the winding Arkansas roads, my husband began to discuss business. I quickly became bored with the discussion, wanting the weekend to be more personal. Then the thought from my meditation came to mind. Was I letting every thought be positive? The answer was no. I changed my negative thoughts to positive ones, and began to appreciate him and this time together.

Throughout this trip, I monitored my thoughts closely to see how positive they were. The weekend turned out like magic. Everything I asked for I got. I wanted seafood salad and there it was on a lunch buffet. I wanted to go on a dinner cruise, and found they had one that night. I wanted to dance and the cruise had live music.

The real miracle of positive thinking happened later that night when I wanted to dance. I grew up dancing and loved it. My husband, as wonderful as he was, did not dance. In the nine years we had been married, we never danced. When I visualized the cruise earlier that day, I saw us dancing. I knew this was something I wanted to experience. I held only positive thoughts in my mind and asked him to dance. He didn't even hesitate. It was truly a miracle.

I came home with a renewed interest in metaphysics. This school obviously knew some things I didn't. I wanted to return to class but was a little embarrassed to call. Knowing Terri, the director, was highly intuitive, I began to send her the mental message to call me. When that didn't happen, I finally picked up the phone and called her. She had been receiving my mental request, but felt it was important I make the decision on my own.

I returned to the school staying for the next year and a half. Even though I was mostly learning about myself at the time, I was also learning about intuition. My sensitivity was becoming more sophisticated. My meditation became more like a full conversation, back and forth between me and whatever it was I was communicating with. At the time I called it God. The information was accurate and never let me down.

THE EXERCISES

What so many people do not understand is that intuition can be learned. It does require some specific mental skills however. The intuitive signal is received and interpreted at a very subtle level. The more concentration, focus, and sensitivity one develops, the more you are capable of receiving this information. Of course objectivity is important as well, or the information will be colored to suit what you want it to say.

The school had a very rigid program. Attendance at the

28

weekly classes was only one small part. There were daily exercises that increased as the course progressed. Before leaving the school, I was up to six hours of exercises per day. I did them devotedly. My mental concentration greatly improved. By the time I left the school, my mind was primed for intuition.

The exercises taught me to be very disciplined. There were several that enhanced concentration and focus at the onset of the classes. Undivided attention was highly stressed, in order to maintain a high level of connection with the subtleties of the inner signals. As time went by, the number of exercises increased. Adding to the mix were breathing, acupuncture point, and memory exercises. We kept a dream journal as well as a meditation journal. This way we had a record of our progress. There was a book assignment weekly, and a report to be written. Further along in the program, dietary changes had to be made. Meditation went from a twenty minute morning exercise, to one morning and afternoon meditation, plus a twenty minute hong sau breathing mediation. We learned to control our pulse and other natural body rhythms as well.

It was a very involved program, keeping the average person at a distance, due to time obligations. Besides the exercises and reading required, there was the weekly class, and after a time, there was a second night of volunteer teaching required. Two weekends a month there was the expectation to attend meetings at the college. One was a two day teachers meeting, and the other a work weekend, helping to maintain the farm and college campus. I enjoyed the school, but when I left, it was very nice to have my life back.

ENTER THE TRANCE

After leaving the school, I wanted to do something different with my life. Certainly my concept of the world had changed. They had introduced me to a new spiritual point of view, and I wanted to share this with others. I decided to attend a professional training program to be certified as a hypnotherapist. This gave me a way to serve others and use what I had learned.

My hypnosis training took the form of an internship that lasted four months. I observed my instructor perform numerous sessions on every topic you can imagine. On top of observing hypnosis, he would take me into a trance state as well. Because of my prior training at the school, I could enter a very deep state quickly.

The hypnotic state was different from the familiar meditative state I was accustomed to. The meditation was directed more outward and upward from the spine, where hypnosis took me down and within. It felt deeper and I didn't experience the electrical sensations I did in meditation. There was a subtle, but noticeable difference, between them.

After completing my internship and being certified as a hypnotherapist, I opened a practice. Mostly I did sessions for weight loss and quitting smoking. I preferred deeper sessions on things like phobias, regressions, and anxieties, but those were few and far between.

It was the early 90's and regression was becoming very popular at the time. A large part of my clientele came for this purpose. I became known as the regressionist in my community. I had no proof these memories were real, but the sessions did seem very therapeutic. There was something about describing these scenes that helped my clients assimilate their current life experiences.

I had my practice for about a year when I was approached to teach hypnosis. I decided to put together a thirty six hour basic program. It made me define what I was experiencing, and I quickly realized I enjoyed teaching.

I was teaching my second hypnosis class, when I met a young woman, who later proved to be a strong initiator of my intuitive skills. Her name was Dee. She was young, around twenty five, but had far more years of study than I in metaphysics. Her long shiny hair was bouncy, which matched her personality. She was very charismatic, with a contagious laugh, that could make most anything seem humorous. She was also very intelligent and well versed in many subjects.

Dee, Dave, and a doctor friend named Rah, all enrolled in the same class. Dee was a natural at hypnosis, and I found it very easy to go under to her voice. She and I had many of the same interests and started doing hypnotic work together outside of class time. We were able to go very deep in trance, with one another, making the sessions more productive.

My next class was filled with college students. Brian was a blond, attractive accounting major who enjoyed theater on the side. He was dramatic and talented with a great sense of humor. When Dee and Brian met, they became instant friends. They were both highly intuitive, had an interest in theater, and both enjoyed hypnosis. They both had an above average curiosity in intuition as did I. That was their reason for taking the course in hypnosis. One day I suggested we use hypnosis to explore our intuitive abilities. They both jumped on the opportunity. The only challenge to this was getting them to stop joking long enough to take the work seriously.

OPENING DOORS

Brian acted as the hypnotic conductor. I went into the trance state, while Dee observed and asked questions. Our goal was to explore what information lay beneath the surface of our awareness. In other words, we were looking to connect with that intuitive network of information.

We had no idea how to get to this information. The only examples I had were those put forth from the metaphysical school I had attended. They proposed the concept of guides as our connection to this intuitive information. Given that none of us had a better plan, we decided to seek help from the guide realm.

As Brian took me under hypnosis, he invited a guide to take me to the informational records that would answer our questions. In the first session, I met a male guide who led me to a library. He wore long robes and looked like some character out of a biblical dream. I was seated at a table and directed to wait there. As Brain continued to ask questions, a movie like image began to come to my mind. With each question he asked, the scene changed relative to the question. I described in great detail the images I saw, along with the thoughts and emotions of each person in the scene.

I was describing a life from the past. It was an easy area in which to start our project. Granted, it was impossible to prove our information correct, leaving it all ambiguous. Nonetheless, it was fun to recount the images in front of my mind. I was very skeptical, however, of my ability to really see anything from the past.

The three of us met weekly to practice. Brian would take me under hypnosis and I would describe the scenes as they came to my mind. The guides changed, the location of the records changed, and the scenes changed with each session.

Our purpose remained the same. We were seeing how much information we could access. Our model was the readings I had observed at the metaphysical school. The years of mental exercises were now paying off. My mind was able to retrieve information, even though I was leery of it all being real. Vague past life scenes weren't enough to convince me of anything.

About a month into our practice sessions, we decided to invite other people to meet with us. Frankly, we were running out of things to ask about one another. We set up a regular Sunday evening meeting with an open invitation to the public. People I knew and those I didn't came to my home. They came to ask questions of my intuitive mind. Brian was at his peak of performance at every session. I was going deeper and deeper each week, getting more and more details. We were having a really good time exploring.

At the end of two months we hit gold, convincing me this was real. It happened one night when a lady handed Brian a piece of paper filled with questions about her life. He folded the paper in half and set it aside. He proceeded to take me into a hypnotic trance, and guided me to the answers to her questions.

I began speaking immediately. This was unusual, because I usually waited for him to prompt me with questions. He didn't even have the chance to unfold the paper before words flowed from my mouth. I covered the fact that she had no children and how she felt about this. I went into her career choices and disappointments for not choosing another direction. I described how she wanted to be a performer and could not. I told her about her resentments in life, and how she felt about her current relationship. I covered every question on the paper.

It was as though a speaker had been turned on with no hesitation in my voice. The sentences were punctuated in just the right places. I felt like I became the information, not just translating something for her. It was so easy, because there was no separation between my mind and her life. It was as though I had merged with this woman for a short time.

When I came out of the session, I looked at the woman who seemed very surprised. She assumed I had read her questions before going into the trance but I had not. Brian nor I knew what she had written on the paper, yet the answers came to my mind anyway. I did not know this woman well enough to have this information about her. The only answer was it came from my intuition.

This was a real turning point for me. The information was easier to access and flowed much faster after this. We were all amazed. We set out to know more about our minds and discovered the keys to our intuition. Each week, we proved we could not only access intuitive information, but it could be done consistently. I had crossed a threshold. I now knew I was intuitive. I had a new resource to use in my life. I could go directly to the information, and it was proving itself to be accurate most of the time.

MOVING ON TO THINGS

I was first introduced to the term remote viewing at a conference. The presentation was on the Russian remote viewing program where they had used only their minds to view submarines and spy on enemy bases. I knew it required the same skill as what I was calling intuition, but it was being used for very practical purposes, viewing places and physical objects. It had never occurred to me to look at physical things in this way. I was impressed with the idea and wanted to know more.

I came home with great curiosity. By this time, my friends Brian and Dee had moved on in life, and I didn't have them to work with me. I had to figure out a way to do remote viewing alone. The idea quickly came to mind to remote view houses.

The phone book proved to be my best resource for this project. I randomly opened to a residential page and picked out an address. If there was a phone number at the address, I assumed there was also a house. I picked an address, and wrote it down on a piece of paper. Seated on the sofa, I repeated the address to myself while going into a deep hypnotic state. I directed my mind, to look only at the outside of the house, not wanting to invade anyone's privacy.

My first image was a baby blue colored home. I looked at it, a little puzzled, because the color was odd. Then a strong feeling came over me. It just didn't feel like this was the right address. It was so strong I erased the image from my mind, repeated the address again, and started over.

This time I saw a close up image of white painted brick. I was so close to the image I could see the dried paint runs. The white brick went halfway up the front of the house, typical of homes built in the sixties. I moved away from the house and saw a black roof, picture window, white siding, a sidewalk that led from the driveway to the front porch with green grassy carpet, and a white metal post. There was a one car garage on the right side of the house, and one well shaped tree in the front yard. A birdhouse hung in the tree with a small half moon opening in front. I was looking at a small ranch style home. It felt like I was in the middle of the road looking right at the house. It was amazing how clear the images were.

I came out of the trance and jotted down all the information. I made note of the baby blue house as well. Later that day, I drove by the address taking my notes with me.

As I approached the home, I caught sight of a baby blue house on my left. Thinking this was the house, I checked the address. It was just a few numbers off. The house I had remotely viewed earlier that day was right next door.

I stopped the car in front of the correct home comparing

35

my notes with the real thing. I went down the list item by item. Only two things were wrong. The siding color was a light gray rather than white as I had seen. The one car garage was on the left rather than the right. Everything else was exactly as I had seen in the remote viewing session.

This worked so well I decided to do it daily. I gathered addresses from the phone book of homes all over the city. I deliberately picked streets I didn't know in unfamiliar neighborhoods. I didn't want to remote view a memory, but view homes I had never seen before.

The project was very beneficial. I was consistent with the skill and able to do it at any time. The research gave me a way to measure my accuracy rate which was quite high at eighty five percent. Even though most sessions were right, I found when I was off, I was completely off. I either saw it all correct, or I didn't even get close to seeing the right house.

Unlike reading a person's thoughts or a past life, remote viewing houses was a way of knowing if my intuition was correctly working. There was no room for interpretation. Either the image was right or it was wrong. I gained confidence as the weeks went by and my skill held true. I continued doing several remote viewing sessions a week for about a year. I had enough data to recognize I was good at this. The proof I needed was now established in my mind.

Chapter Four

THE SKILL APPLIED

WORKING AS AN INTUITIVE

I put a great deal of effort into developing my intuition, but had no goals of application along the way. Once I realized how well it was functioning, I felt a sense of obligation to do something useful with it. The challenge was figuring out how to fit this into my life.

I was a real estate investor before the transition to full time intuitive consultant came about. The world of real estate was very good to me, and I could easily have continued focusing in that direction. I was knowledgeable in the field, enjoyed it very much, and it had been a long time dream. Shifting my focus so drastically from real estate to spiritual work seemed very important at the time, even though it was a radical step.

I have always been interested in helping people and even considered becoming a psychologist at one time. I like solving problems, enjoy seeing people reach their potential, and like being on the cutting edge of new discovery. I recognized my intuitive abilities were very strong, and even though I wasn't working professionally with my intuition, I knew I could. When I finally made the decision, it was for two reasons. One, I wanted to spiritually grow, and by plunging head first into this line of work,

I knew I would grow the most. The second reason was because I felt I could help others, and that made my life purposeful.

The decision was not an easy one. It certainly wasn't financially driven, for it was far less income than anything I had ever done. My ego wasn't boosted either, for my self-esteem dropped. Most people I knew looked at this as a real step down. So between the lack of income and the loss of prestige in my self-identity, it is a wonder I did it at all. Clearly, I made the decision out of a deep love for the work, rather than selfish gain.

The benefits from this line of work came from the sessions themselves rather than money or ego. I learned about life, spirit, and myself, each time I connected with that intuitive state. Being of a very curious mind, I also continued to explore and discover how intuition, the physical world, and thought, fit together. The work itself was very satisfying, and I never regretted the move.

I have explored an endless number of topics with my clients, and still find it fascinating when the right answer is intuitively discovered. The rewards of seeing health problems disappear, finding lost items for people, and seeing relationships improve have exceeded all expectations. I know of no other profession that could possibly have given me this type of insight.

My work invites me into people's personal lives. I understand their needs and witness their benefits. The examples that follow are not the dramatic cases I have worked with, those will come later in the book. What I want to show here is the reality of my occupation. It is the real life situations that keep me closely tied to the work.

PETS

Occasionally, I am asked to do a health session for

someone's pet. I am not a pet owner, but have come to experience the deep love my clients have for the animals in their lives. A pet becomes part of the family. There is concern for the animal when it is in pain.

A devoted client from another state called one day asking that I take a look at her cat. It didn't matter that I had never seen the cat because this skill is not based on physical vision. She had been told by a veterinarian the cat suffered from fleas. The owner didn't believe this because it was an indoor cat and she had never seen a flea on her. Whatever it was caused the cat to scratch one hip until her hair came off. The poor cat's hip was raw and irritated.

I saw several things contributing to this, one, that the cat had been injured as a kitten. She had an odd walk, kind of side ways. The nerves were damaged in that hip where the injury had occurred. I could tell the cat had a tingling sensation in her skin that caused her to scratch until the hair came off

She was also allergic to Styrofoam. The sofa cushions, carpet pad, and numerous other things in the house had Styrofoam in the fiber. The poor cat was suffering every time she rubbed her raw skin up against the contaminated items. I suggested cotton towels or other natural materials be used to create a safer and more comfortable environment for the cat. There were some products that could be rubbed on her skin to help keep the irritation down as well. I could feel the suffering of the small animal throughout the session, and felt a great deal of compassion for her.

When I finished, the owner was eager to try some of the suggestions. She could easily place cotton towels down for the cat to lay on, but keeping her off the carpet posed more of a challenge. She also verified the cat had always had this funny sideways walk but she never knew why.

She called a few weeks later telling me how much the cat had improved. Keeping her raw irritated skin off the Styrofoam fibers had helped considerably. The cat was no longer scratching the hair from her hip but continued to walk sideways. There was very little that could be done about the injury but the cat was more comfortable. Both the owner and the cat were relieved.

CHRONIC ISSUES

A woman came to me with a chronic pain on the right side of her neck that had bothered her for years. No treatment had helped rid her of this, even though she had sought out many traditional and nontraditional therapies.

After intuitively looking at the issue, I found what was causing the pain. She had a favorite chair where she sat in the evenings. She propped her head up with one hand causing the neck to be in a tilted position. This forced the neck to be slightly twisted. It was a relaxing position for her, but it made the neck and spine move out of place. The pain occurred over and over because she continued to sit in this way.

She confirmed this was her usual sitting position in the evenings while watching television or reading. Once she realized this was the problem, however, she altered it, immediately correcting the issue. The pain went away and did not return. Sometimes it is the simplest of solutions that resolves a problem.

FAMILY

I enjoy doing family sessions and it is just as easy to intuitively connect with a group as one person. I once did a session for a woman and her two children. She was a busy single mother with little time spent with her young daughter and son. She wanted to make the most of their precious, youthful years.

Her motivation was to find the most valuable activities they could share.

I went into the session with no knowledge of her children as this was the first time I had met the woman. I wanted to give the children a voice so I connected with all three of them. I asked each what they needed most from one another. The children agreed that doing simple fun things, like playing games, was the most joy they had with their mother. Getting down on the floor, on their level, playing pretend, was what they really liked.

When I stated this, the mother was surprised. She was a bit extravagant and liked taking them out to big productions. I assured her they did enjoy those things but the real bonds between them were formed when they simply had her attention. This happened in simple, playful settings around the house.

Parents sometimes have no idea what a child wants from them. Often it is difficult for a child to say what they need. I am very impressed when children intuitively speak with me. If I can help bridge the communication between parent and child, my job is well done.

I once did a session for a six year old with a physical disorder, prohibiting her from growing normally. When I told her parents I would give the child a voice, tears started running down the mother's face, she was so emotionally touched. In her daughters six years of life, she had never been able to speak with them.

It was interesting to see how the child had matured despite her physical handicaps. She requested her parents give her more responsibility, even though it was difficult given her limitations. The parents were giving her wonderful care, but had failed to see she was now six, and not two. Her mind and body were growing even though she was unable to reach a state of independence. She needed to be treated in a more mature way.

They began a new program of interaction with her. Their language took on a more adult manner. They let her do more things for herself, encouraging her to try new things that would make her feel more independent. She became more content and their relationship with her improved.

MARRIAGE

Troubled relationships are everywhere, but I often see them up close and personal, as an intuitive consultant. When two people are thinking of dissolving a long term relationship, confusion can set in around the question of what to do. They will often seek help through an intuitive session at this time.

I often feel the love beneath the surface of a troubled marriage, but there are obstacles in the way of showing this love to one another. Open and honest dialog is often difficult in their communication with one another due to negative habitual exchange. This is where I come in. By going straight to the heart of each person, I say what they can not. Sometimes I see little can be done to save the situation and others appear to be salvageable.

In one session, the term emotional braiding was advised for a couple that had little intimacy. I saw a process of each person giving emotionally, creating a strong braid of energy between them. The emotional braid was so strong little could ever pull it apart. More than the strength of the braid, was the happiness this would enable the two to experience. Later, I looked at a simple step by step procedure to help this braiding occur which involved communicating through eye contact, touching, and sharing dreams with one another.

I had a friend once who was debating on a divorce. She

had four children, one, being a thirteen year old daughter, whom the mother often confided in about her feelings. After a session with the woman, the daughter started appearing in my dreams. She told me how she was torn apart by her mother's confessions. She loved both her mother and father, and wanted to be supportive to both of them, but could not directly tell her mother.

I shared the daughter's message with the mother. Her daughter was too young to understand the complications of her parents' adult relationship. The mother was simply expecting more of the thirteen year old than she could give. I was glad to see the mother understood and ceased talking with her daughter about her marital problems.

LOOKING FOR JUST THE RIGHT PERSON

Not all relationship sessions are about problems. Sometimes they involve looking into the future for just the right person. Julie came to me several times before she met her mister right. I heard the name Adam over and over as the name of the person she would meet. She was skeptical, since she had been single all of her life, and was a mature woman. With an open mind, she continued to look for him, just in case he was out there somewhere.

Just before Julie met Adam, I described his life in an intuitive session. I described him as being very literary, a strong demeanor and physique, fairly tall and slender, normal straight hair, and well tanned. He worked in some governmental administrative position.

I went on to say he was often very close to her but they just didn't meet. I saw something purple and green set on a white background. That seemed important regarding this but I didn't know why. Julie listened but I could tell she was a bit skeptical.

Several months later Julie was thinking about moving. I had described her mother's move, with much accuracy, so she wanted me to do the same for her. The information she was seeking was about where and when this move might take place. She wanted to know her options.

I saw her moving in the fall during the month of October. It would be ten miles due south of her current home. The new place was surrounded by trees and it felt as though she were enclosed in a warm, safe, comfortable environment. It seemed like a very positive move for her and she would be happy there.

At the end of the session, she asked again about a relationship. I continued to see her with Adam. Even though I could not remember the description I gave before, I gave her the same information again.

A few weeks later Julie called with the news of meeting a man by the name of Adam. She was very excited, knowing from my description, this was the one. He had the same type of job, body description, was very literary, and his house was exactly ten miles due south of her home. It was a beautiful place surrounded by trees like the home I had described. She didn't know him well enough to say she would be moving in by October, but they were very happy.

Just as I had seen in the session, the two of them had been within close range of one another for some time and not met. Adam's sister lived right across from the school where Julie taught. He visited his sister each Wednesday placing him within very close range of Julie each week. They had practically been running into each other for years.

Once they got to know each other, Adam took Julie to meet this sister who was known in the family for her beautiful quilting. One of her prize quilts was spread out on a bed facing a window looking directly at Julie's school. It was made up of gorgeous purple and green blocks. These were the two colors significant in the intuitive session to their near meetings.

I had seen this relationship coming for some time and now here it was. Julie was so happy. She honestly felt she had found the person of her dreams. In October that year Julie moved in with Adam, on track with the move I had seen in her life months before. At the time I looked at Julie's move, I had no idea it would be connected with Adam since he wasn't even in the picture yet. His home was obviously what I was viewing because it was exactly ten miles due south. It was also surrounded by trees, creating that warm home like feeling I shared in the earlier session.

Happy endings do occur. Today Julie and Adam are married. They were the perfect match for one another and very compatible. When the time was right they met. What a wonderful love story to see in advance.

Only occasionally is a romance as intuitively clear as Julie and Adams. This one just hit the mark. I often look at the romantic side of a person's life and see very little. I describe all opportunities I see coming along even if they are vague. Most of them are unclear and feel uncertain, which makes me think they may not happen.

I knew both Julie and Adam were seriously looking for a relationship. They had so much in common that drew them together. They were ready for one another. When a person has not been focusing on a relationship, it shows up as uncertainty in an intuitive session. There is very little energy built around that part of their lives. In that case, I have little or nothing to tell them. If they are thinking in negative terms about a relationship, it repels rather than draws the right person to them. That is reflected as short term relationships that do not work out. I try to help people understand how their thoughts and feelings make a difference.

DIRECT MIND COMMUNICATION

It was nearly 6:15 p.m. when I stirred the rice on the stove and attended to the final details of the evening meal. As I looked at my watch I questioned if my friend Paula would be late again as she almost always was. Being certain she would be, the question then moved on to how late. I decided to connect with her mind directly and find out.

She was to arrive at 6:30 p.m. but as I looked at my watch I realized it was already that time. I intuitively connected with Paula's mind and simply asked her what time she would arrive. I heard in a clear voice, that sounded exactly like hers, I should be there by 6:45.

I had used this process long enough to trust it. I made the final preparations to the meal while I waited the fifteen minutes for her arrival. At exactly 6:45 p.m. the doorbell rang. Confident it was her, I walked to the door to find her waiting on the other side. As she entered the room, I smiled and explained the conversation we had at 6:30. She laughed, as Paula often did, and told me she looked at her watch at 6:30, and distinctly remembered having the thought I should be there by 6:45.

It was not uncommon for Paula and I to communicate in this way. It was also not uncommon for me to initiate this kind of communication with others. I often ask people questions directly even when they are not in my presence. When I hear a clear distinct voice, sounding like their own, I know I have a clear intuitive answer.

The way Paula and I communicate intuitively is the same way I communicate in my professional sessions. When someone has a question about how a relative, an employer, or a friend may respond to a choice they are considering, I intuitively ask them. If they do not want the person to know, the answer is very limited. Many times, however, they are more than willing to share this information and a few times it has turned into a lecture.

Once a woman asked about a situation between her son and husband who did not see eye to eye on some issues. When intuitively asked, the husband had a great deal to say. Having done numerous sessions for this man in the past, I knew this must be important to him because he usually shared very little. The information was good, giving all of them a direction to go in resolving the family friction that had been building for awhile.

MUTUAL FEELINGS

When an intuitive session is helpful, it makes my work very satisfying. There is a warmth that fills my emotions. Sometimes it is years before I hear about the benefits of a session I have done. I will receive a note or a call from someone thanking me for how much the information helped, and sometimes even changed their entire path of life.

I look at what I do as problem solving. There is usually a desire on the part of my client to find an answer to some situation they are facing. It may be in the area of health, relationships, or just self-understanding. It really doesn't matter what it is because intuition works the same on any subject. My job is to remain focused and retrieve an answer. The answer should give them clarity about the subject. Most often it will reflect what they already know, but are afraid to look at directly.

I have never regretted my choice to become a full time intuitive. The gratitude and respect I have for my clients is mutual. The depth of understanding human nature has superceded any expectations I could ever have had when I began

47

this work. I feel highly blessed and rewarded for my choice.

Chapter Five

MIND DEVELOPED

ADVANCED USE OF INTUITION

That gut feeling or hunch that comes along occasionally is often referred to as intuition. As I speak of intuition in this book, I want to clarify that even though the gut feeling and hunch are intuitive, they represent the simplest form. The skill, as I use it and teach others, is far more complex than a random hunch. It is a learned process of searching for answers to very specific questions.

The advanced use of intuition takes the vague intuitive impression and defines its meaning. The meaning must relate to the subject of the question, or it will be an ambiguous answer. That is why an advanced intuitive session must have specific boundaries of topic in order to produce the desired results.

As an example, I was asked to locate a lost passport for a woman who was leaving the country the next day. She only realized it was missing the night before, and became desperate searching her office from top to bottom. Frantic when she couldn't find it, she called me. She felt it was among the many items in her office, but had no idea where. My job was to find the passport.

With the advanced skill of intuition, I was able to locate the passport. This was done by narrowing my intuitive perception, singularly to the passport itself, and then describing the surroundings which led her to it.

I could see the passport had fallen down between some other papers in a dark, tight congested area. It was midway up in the room which meant there was no purpose in looking high on a shelf or under a table. I then saw something that looked like an old English scene. There were men with white wigs dressed in long tailed red coats. The furnishings around them looked like something from the 1880's. As I described this to her, she was puzzled and felt certain this could not have anything to do with the location of her passport, assuming I was seeing her upcoming trip to England.

After some encouragement, she continued to look through her office. She discovered a picture hanging above her file cabinet with the old English scene. She opened the file cabinet drawer and began looking between files where she found her passport.

Advanced intuition focuses on finding answers to resolve problems. You must be able to direct your focus with great precision, and retrieve only information that pertains to the situation. An unskilled intuitive will often access unrelated pieces of information. They will also let their attention drift, losing the single mindedness needed to remain focused. Much like reading a book by flipping from one section to the next and back to the front, the information may relate to the subject, but it is disjointed and lacks meaning.

The advanced intuitive must constantly monitor their awareness. They need to keep the subject of the session in mind at all times, and interpret the information that comes to them in a meaningful way, as it relates to the questions. In other words, the intuitive's focus must remain in balance with the goal of the session. The ability to do this is the basic difference between the advanced use of the intuitive skill and random intuitive perception.

Another example of advanced intuition is shown by Angela Thompson Smith, author of *Remote Perceptions.* She was given a target of the Unabomber back in 1995 before the public knew of him. The information she received was later handed over to the FBI and was found to be very accurate. She was able to intuitively perceive and describe his physical body, living conditions, personality traits, educational background, and emotional state with no knowledge of this person.

I worked on a case finding a fugitive in my home area some years ago. He had evaded capture for several days, stealing automobiles, breaking into rural houses, and even killing several people. By focusing my attention at a point of his last known crime, I followed his trail across mid Missouri going east. I got the number of the highway he traveled on going south to the boot heel area of the state. I then saw him cross the Mississippi River where he stopped at a small, inexpensive motel across the river in Illinois to rest. I could see a billboard near the motel with a religious advertisement. The next morning they captured him just across the Missouri line in Illinois near the boot heel of Missouri. He was staying at a small motel near the Mississippi River.

Unfortunately, I could not take credit for his capture because this information never reached the authorities. It did show a level of accuracy in tracking the path of a person, however.

ADVANCED INTUITION IN CRIMINAL CASES

I have worked on two murder cases in my career. In both

instances, I was hired by a family member and not law enforcement. The information I received intuitively in both cases, fit what was known of the crime.

CASE #1

A woman came for a session regarding the murder of her sister. It was an unsolved crime that occurred in California several years prior. She wanted to know who murdered her sister and why. I asked her not to give me any further information so I would not be consciously biased with my search for the answer to her question. I focused on the date of the murder and the address where her body was found. I looked moment by moment at her sister's life just before the murder.

I saw her leave her house, turn right, and walk down a sidewalk late in the afternoon to early evening. She followed the sidewalk around a curve in the street. Her journey ended as she stopped at a sign near a much busier intersection. While standing at the stop sign, she was confronted by three young men in a car. I described each of the three men. They looked very intimidating and had a rough appearance.

I then saw them step out of the car and attack the woman. I felt the blows to her body as they brutally beat her. The weight of her body felt heavy as she collapsed to the ground. They left her to die in some bushes near the intersection.

I described the surroundings of this area as residential with houses lining the street. A vacant field lay across the road. A busy freeway was just beyond the intersection to the right.

Her sister shared the points of accuracy she knew about the case.

- Her sister was beaten to death.

- Body found near a stop sign at a busy intersection.
- Body found in bushes.
- Stop sign led to a busy street.
- Vacant field across street.
- Major freeway to the right just beyond intersection.
- Houses lined the street leading to this intersection.
- One turn in direction along this road.
- Gang members suspected murderers.

The deceased woman was a witness to some gang activity and was to testify in court. The police suspected she was murdered before she was able to testify against them, but did not have enough evidence to arrest any of the gang members. After finding out more, I went back to look for an eye witness or any evidence that would help the case. I did not find anyone witnessing this murder nor any item of evidence that could now be found.

CASE #2

A woman whose father had been murdered asked that I look at the circumstances surrounding this event. I started the session only knowing the address and date of the murder.

My intuitive focus was on describing step by step the events of the evening. The first scene showed a car pulling up in front of the house and a rather large man dressed in white get out and go to the door. From this, I saw a confrontation occur between him and the victim. The man left the house and drove off.

As the night progressed, I saw several people come and go from the residence. There was a woman with two small children who were there for some time. There was a young man with baggy pants, wearing a baseball cap, who came by for a short time and then left.

I jumped to the moment of the murder and saw the man's body on the kitchen floor surrounded by blood. Beside him was a red and white flip top cooler. As I moved my focus through the house, I saw three bullet holes in the ceiling of the bedroom. I knew this was an area of confrontation.

The woman and children were not present at the time of the murder nor was the young man with the baseball cap. The man dressed in white had returned later in the evening, I believed, and shot the woman's father.

After the session, the woman told me what she knew of that evening. The police found her father's body in a pool of blood on the kitchen floor. She knew he owned a small red and white cooler, but had no idea if it was in the kitchen that evening. There were three bullet holes discovered in the bedroom ceiling during the police investigation. Neighbors testified a woman with two small children had been at the house that evening. It was thought they had left long before the murder occurred.

The young man with the baseball cap was there that evening, and was arrested for the murder. The unknown part was, if the man in the white coat was there, as I had seen. She knew who he was, and even suspected him to be the murderer, but had no proof.

To this day, I believe the police arrested the wrong man for the murder. I specifically saw him come and go from the house with no confrontation, whereas the man in the white coat was at the house twice that evening in an agitated state.

We were never able to prove if my version of the murder was correct. However, I saw each item correctly that was known, leading me to believe the rest was as well. We will never know for sure.

TESTING ADVANCED INTUITION

In a research project designed to test the advanced skill of intuition, a group of six looked at New York Stock Exchange stock values over a period of time. Three new stocks were viewed each week, and the names were unknown to the viewers until after the sessions were complete. This was done by assigning the stock a random number.

The viewers were to focus on one stock at a time and see if it increased in value by twenty percent over the next sixty days. A record was kept of the value of the stock at the time of viewing, and over the next sixty days, to determine if the correct answer was yes or no.

At the end of six months, the group's accuracy rate was sixty-five percent, with some in the group, including myself, being at eighty-five percent correct.

In other test sessions, I looked at future events of individuals over the span of a week. The events were random, with the intuitive focus being on a verifiable moment, occurring on a specified date. The scenes were documented, but not shared with the individual until after the week was over. Eighty percent of the future scenes I viewed for this class happened. Here are some of them.

I saw a woman in her kitchen along with her husband on a Wednesday afternoon. A bee was swarming around the room causing a frantic emotional state in both of them. I saw her swatting at the bee, trying desperately to persuade it to exit the house through an open door. This had occurred as seen.

On Thursday morning, there is a disturbing sound waking another woman from a sound sleep. The sound is generated from outside the home and is a roaring motorized type of noise. The woman continues to try and sleep, but is kept awake by the on going sound. She confirmed this happened, and it was a neighbor running a weed eater near the bedroom window.

A woman is seen separating and stacking small groups of coins on a Tuesday evening. She cleaned out her purse and organized the loose change found in the bottom of the bag on that very night.

On a Friday afternoon, a woman is seen looking at her toes and then looking at her hands. This process of focus, between the toes and hands, went back and forth several times. She confirmed this did occur. During a conversation at work about feet, she and a co-worker kicked off their shoes and compared toes followed by the comparison of hands. This was repeated several times before going back to work.

Even though these scenes were very brief moments, they included enough specific information to separate them from other events. The fact that they were time specific helped to establish the validity of the information as well.

These are examples of testing the advance skill of intuition. In more practical applications, it has been used to assist in archeological digs, legal matters, and in resolving mechanical issues.

I have used it many times in child custody cases and criminal trials. I look at the judge or jury, observing their attitudes, to help in determining the best direction to go with a case.

Chapter Six

INTUITION INSPIRES HEALING

HEALTH INTUITIVE

My specialty today is as a health intuitive. I am certain my first health intuitive session by the metaphysical school played some part in this choice. It gave me insight in how my thoughts and emotions influenced my physical state. My health and over all attitudes improved upon applying their suggestions.

Even though I never intended to be a health intuitive, when I began to do professional sessions, it sort of made its way to the front of my practice. There were two reasons why I was reluctant to do health sessions when I began. One I had no medical training, and two I didn't want to harm anyone. As fate would have it, it turned out to be my area of specialty.

SPONTANEOUS HEALTH INTUITIVE SESSION

Early in my new profession as an intuitive, I opened a shop in a small artistic community. I sold books, antiques, and did short intuitive sessions in order to enhance my intuitive abilities. Margaret, a local resident, called one Saturday evening wanting a session right away. Even though we had never met, a mutual friend had highly recommended me. I set the appointment for the following evening when the shop would be closed.

Normally, I did my intuitive sessions in the back of the store, but because I wasn't open for business this evening, I decided to use a table near the front. I walked by a small, decorative crystal ball on a stand, and felt compelled to move it to the table where I would be doing the session. As I walked toward the front of the store with the crystal ball in hand, I criticized myself for looking like a gypsy, crystal ball reader. I never used devices like this to be intuitive. I had learned to directly link with my intuitive state, and that was all I ever needed. Even so, I found myself placing the crystal ball on the table.

Margaret arrived, and I was amazed at how beautiful she looked with dark eyes and a glowing tanned complection. Her cheery disposition jumped out from her openly friendly smile. She was looking for answers about a legal situation in her life. The session lasted for almost an hour, as we covered every aspect of the problem. When it ended she hesitated and then asked if I knew anything about guardian angels. She wanted me to contact her guardian angel if I could.

I had no idea how to contact a guardian angel, but then I had no idea how to be intuitive when I first started all of this either. All I could do was give it a try.

Uncertain what to do, I depended on my inner guidance to show me. At that moment, my eyes went to the crystal ball on the table. I intuitively knew to pick it up and hold it between both hands. As I closed my eyes to enter the intuitive state, I suddenly felt a strong sensation moving up my arms. It was a tingling like feeling that continued until it reached my heart. I then felt the most incredible sense of compassion.

Suddenly words began to flow from my mouth. The advice coming through me was directed toward Margaret's health. I was unaware of any illness she might have. She certainly didn't look unhealthy. Yet, the words continued to flow regarding her need for dietary and life style changes along with rest. She needed to stop many of the activities that took away from her energy, and start doing things to help her recuperate. The session went on to address her need for self-love and other emotional aspects of her life that were missing.

I spoke on and on for another fifteen minutes until the session felt complete and the words stopped flowing. When I opened my eyes, Margaret was staring at me in disbelief. She had a disability that had taken her from a very lucrative position as a CPA to living on a meager income in this small town. Even though she did not show the discomfort in her face, she was in constant pain, seldom slept, and was unable to work. She was ignoring her basic needs, making the situation worse with each day. My words had spoken a truth to her she knew I could not have known.

Margaret was my first health intuitive session. It was totally spontaneous and unintended. I wasn't sure what I did, but I had tapped into something that was very powerful and accurate. This experience changed my view of doing health sessions. Margaret's session described her symptoms very well. The advice was very sensible and harmless.

Meanwhile a friend of mine, Gary, also wanted a health intuitive session. I agreed to do this but only for practice. I immediately saw a curve in his spinal column that did not look normal. I described the image I saw, and then told him how to best compensate for the problem. Gary looked at me and smiled. No one had ever seen the curve in his spine without the aid of an x-ray before now.

Even though both sessions had been very accurate, I was still in conflict about offering them as part of my regular work. On one hand, I was encouraged by the results of the two sessions. On the other hand, I knew my intuition could be wrong. I decided to develop a structure giving the sessions more of a spiritual base than physical. It included describing the body but mostly it was about the emotions, thought patterns, and spiritual needs, associated with the physical issues.

Once again, I called upon my friend Dee to help. It didn't take long to realize I needed a format to follow while doing the sessions. I played around with several before finally settling on one.

The process evolved into seeing my client as a silhouette in front of me. I scanned the body, starting with the head, moving down to the feet, and back to the head. During the scan, there would be areas of the body that seemed pronounced. I would focus on that area, describe what I saw, and then move on to describe the mental, emotional and spiritual issues associated with this problem. The nice thing about intuitive work is I do not have to be in the presence of the person when I do it. This means I can do sessions for people anywhere in the world.

I never start a session with a preconceived idea about the person. I never know what part of the body I will be drawn to. It may be the knee, the liver, or the thyroid gland. I just let my intuition guide me to the areas needing attention. I describe what I see, but do not diagnose. For instance, I never tell a client they have cancer, heart disease, or diabetes. I will describe irregular looking cell structure, weakened energy in the heart region, or sluggishness in the digestive track. I encourage physical exams by qualified practitioners. For my client's safety, I explain this process is not foolproof. I stress the health intuitive session is

60

intended to be a guide for spiritual growth and not a physical exam.

This is a wholistic process and very spiritual in nature. For each physical issue I see in the body, I relate the emotions, thought patterns, and spiritual needs. The emphasis is on the whole person not just being physically well.

I believe the body is a reflection of the whole being. If there is a physical issue, there will be some emotion, thought, and spiritual balance needed. Sometimes the physical issue will be screaming for my attention as I scan the body, but it is always the spiritual part that has the answer.

SPIRITUAL NOT PHYSICAL

There are many reasons for focusing on the health intuitive session from a spiritual point of view. One is to stay within the framework of the law. I cannot practice medicine nor do I want to. I am not licensed, nor qualified, to give a health diagnosis to anyone.

I am qualified to do intuitive work which is more spiritual in nature. I remotely see into the body and simply describe what I perceive, while connecting to the spiritual part of the person. I often see the physical condition, but I feel the spiritual needs as a void in the person's life. I try and give them information on how to fill this void so healing may occur.

Often the spiritual needs have been ignored for some time before a disease sets in the body. The body is the last place to feel the severity of what we deny our spirit to express. We each have a unique quality. This quality is based in the spirit of our being, and it desires to reach its potential during our lifetime. Through the intuitive sessions, I have been able to see the threads of likeness between all people, as well as this unique spiritual aspect. It is finding that special spiritual part of ourselves and giving that which keeps us most healthy. That is the wholistic approach I express through my health intuitive work. My goal is not just that the person heal, but that the potential of their spirit be recognized and expressed.

I am not saying that everyone who follows their spiritual path will be healthy. What I am saying is you have the most opportunity to be physically well when you are spiritually happy. If some area of your mental, emotional, or spiritual life is troubled, it will eventually reflect in the body as a disorder.

Many times the physical issue is only a messenger of spirit. So often I ignore a painful area of my body. When I am willing to look inside at the greater issue causing the pain, most often it will go away. By accepting responsibility for my condition from a spiritual point of view, the pain has no reason to stay. Thoughts and feelings impact our spiritual expression the most. Just being aware of our thoughts and feelings can help our spiritual expression to change. Sometimes I need to drop a project that no longer serves me or start one that does. And sometimes major life changes, including the way I think and feel about myself, is in order for my spiritual quality to come through.

SELF-BLAME

Some people are offended by the idea they cause their own disease. In Western medicine, disease is about germs, viruses, bacteria, and injury. Never is it about thoughts or feelings or how energy flows through the body. From a wholistic view, it is about all the above. We can not deny the existence of invading bacteria and viruses. But we have been able to deny the influence our thoughts and feelings have on the body.

We have a compartmentalized point of view of ourselves. This makes us see the physical as unrelated to the rest of our being. Disease then, is strictly a physical issue caused by outside influences. This takes responsibility off our shoulders and places it on the world around us. The only responsibility we are left with is to be defensive once an outside invasion occurs. So what is to blame? Is it the invading forces external and beyond our control, or is it the inner climate we set with our thoughts and feelings?

It is both. No one is denying outside forces exist. There is a correlation between exposure to a cold virus and coming down with a cold. But how often have you been exposed to a cold virus and did not come down with a cold? What causes the body to resist a disease or be susceptible to it? If you view yourself from a more wholistic point, you will see it is a combination of factors. Those include the way you think and feel and how you are interpreting your life experience.

By holding onto the idea that disease is something you can do little about, you continue to give that power to forces outside yourself. You do not have to be responsible for your thoughts and feelings as they relate to your health. You can think and feel any way you want and never be blamed.

I once told a bald man there was a thought pattern associated with baldness. While I was attempting to think of what it was, he became very upset. He felt like I was accusing him of somehow being responsible for his hair falling out. Before I had a chance to explain, he started attacking me for daring to blame him.

He had been traumatized when he started losing his hair in his early twenties. This was a real sore spot for him. He thought I was suggesting he could have stopped this from happening by changing his thoughts. He was very offended and believed if there had been any possible way he could have stopped it he would have.

What he didn't understand was that I wasn't blaming him for having this thought pattern. I was only suggesting that baldness, as with all other physical conditions, have certain thought patterns associated with them. These patterns are very subconscious in nature, telling your body how to respond. The wholistic approach does not hold your conscious thinking fully responsible for these patterns. This also doesn't mean every physical disorder in your body will suddenly go away just because you change your conscious thoughts.

There are certain ways of thinking and feeling associated with physical disorders. I refer to these as subconscious patterns of thinking. You should never blame yourself for having these patterns, but rather seek ways to understand and change them to a better, healthier end result.

My personal belief is we all come in with certain patterns of thinking. We have genetic links and environmental influences that shape these patterns. Just as our genetic make up and personal experiences are unique to us, so are our emotional responses and thoughts. We are able to see this clearly by looking at two children growing up in the same household. They have very individual ways of reacting to life.

Our unique patterns of thinking and emotional responses are very subconscious in nature. Most of us are not aware of them at all. Because we are not aware of these deep subconscious patterns, it is often beyond our scope to see them or change them. A health intuitive session may point out these very deep, subconscious patterns. Bringing them to our awareness is the first step in changing them. When the subconscious pattern is truly changed, then the physical body may change as well.

This doesn't mean the bald man will grow hair once his thoughts change. It does mean that the biological factors that caused his hair to fall out may change once the subconscious patterns change.

We are responsible for our physical condition only to the degree we are aware of our subconscious patterns. Could the man have stopped his hair from falling out? We will never know and I would never blame him. I do believe a certain type of personality loses their hair.

One should never beat themselves up for having a disease, but rather start working for a positive change. Let the nature of changing the subconscious patterns help in creating wholeness in the body. The wholistic approach offers insight for the whole person. It is not about blame. It is about self-awareness and change.

When given all the right elements, the body knows how to heal. Understanding the whole person is vital in giving yourself all the right elements. This gives your body the most opportunity for natural healing to occur.

PREVENTION

According to the medical biology research being done today by people like Dr. Bruce Lipton, perception does make a difference in disease. In his book *Biology of Belief,* genetic programming is attributed to our subconscious perception. Genes cannot turn themselves on or off but rather it is a process influenced by the subconscious autonomic system. Subconscious beliefs and perceptions are in charge. Mostly this is at a very deep subconscious level beyond our awareness. The more aware we become, the more we are able to direct these deep subconscious patterns to change.

If our health is so dependent on our subconscious beliefs and perceptions, then why are we not exploring this more fully? Health is as much a perception issue as it is a physical invasion issue. It doesn't matter if you are predisposed to have cancer because your parents did. It doesn't matter if you have a gene for Alzheimers. It only matters if your beliefs and perceptions tell your body to turn that gene on and make it active.

You can change your beliefs and perceptions. You must first become aware of them. That is what the health intuitive process helps you to understand. Knowing we have some influence over our physical condition gives me hope. I am hopeful we may be able to prevent many diseases by working on a subconscious level.

An intuitive session can help you see what you are predisposed to develop. I often will see a disorder forming in a client only to find out later a parent or grandparent suffered from the same condition. By working on changing your beliefs and perceptions at a subconscious level, you have the opportunity to change this predisposed genetic make up.

Wouldn't it be wonderful if we could turn a destructive gene off, rather than believing we must suffer from diabetes, arthritis, or heart disease, just because it runs in the family? For those prone to develop such disorders, it could be a major blessing.

When we learn to think of disease as something we can manage through our inner belief structure, then we will be thinking wholistically. Our thoughts and feelings are constant reflections of our subconscious patterns of thinking. That is why it is important to pay attention to them, because they are influencing the physical body daily.

The thought of being able to change thoughts and beliefs to alter disease is totally foreign to most people. Because Western society does not look at genetic make up as something that can be influenced, it will take some time before this idea will be accepted.

According to Dr. Bruce Lipton, the research on genes today will not be in the medical text books for another fifteen or so years. Until then, medicine will continue to practice in the way it has. We will continue to be taught that we have no real influence over our genetic make up.

Our thoughts and feelings send a message to our body. Many patterns of thinking and responding are very deeply rooted in our subconscious. They come in with us as a pattern or way of thinking. We then shape them through our life experiences. We are each unique in the way we think and express, and yet, many patterns between us are alike.

Those with like beliefs are prone to the same disorders. Louise Hay and Dr. Daniel Condron have written books about the thoughts and feelings associated with certain disorders in the body. These are general descriptions, but good guidelines to understand the body/mind relationship.

A health intuitive session is a wholistic approach to understanding this body/mind relationship. It is not a diagnostic session to heal a disease in your body. It is a way to go deep within your spirit, thoughts, and feelings and take a look at the patterns associated with a particular issue.

My belief is health intuitive sessions are preventive in nature because they can help you see what you are most prone to develop. Often the changes needed are not obvious. The best way to prevent a disorder from developing is to make changes before it happens.

There is not a way to prove you will contract a certain disorder just because you are predisposed to do so. What we do know is you can influence your health through establishing healthy thoughts and emotions. We know intuition allows us to see these deep subconscious patterns both healthy and unhealthy.

There are so many levels to staying healthy. Foods we eat, life style, and general care make a difference. I encourage good physical care of the body as well as healthy thought patterns. The freedom to choose your thoughts and feelings is yours. As a precaution to good health, it pays to know your subconscious thought patterns. These patterns make us prone to certain disorders but this can be changed.

A wholistic plan is preventive, rather than fixing the symptoms, once a disease is present. It can be far more cost effective, as well as aiding you to live a happier and healthier life.

SEEING HEALING

A good friend of mine called one day requesting prayer for her husband who was going into surgery the next day. He had gone in for a regular health exam for the company insurance policy. During the exam, they discovered some blockages and scheduled him for immediate heart surgery.

I did a quick intuitive session for him as was requested. It was too late to do any preventive work, but it was not too late to let the mind/body relationship work for him now. I saw a successful surgery with his recovering in rapid time. I shared this with his wife who was quite worried.

She ask about his guardian angels. As I looked at that intuitively, I saw two. I saw one named Phillip, and another named Gerald. When he awoke in the recovery room, he had two male nurses caring for him. As he read their name badges, he discovered one was named Phillip and the other Gerald. This brought a smile to his face for he knew he was well cared for and all would be fine. He recovered in rapid time.

On the flip side of this, I have also seen death in a person's future. I hold true to the idea things can change and never tell anyone when they will die. I like to give hope in all situations. Sometimes I see when the person will not make changes, and death will most likely occur. In this case, I give a time I see lowered energy in the body. These are important times to pay attention. If change is to be made, it is best to do so before the body energy gets too low.

A man diagnosed with a very progressive cancer came to me one day for a health session. His biggest question was when he would die. He had already accepted this idea as an inevitable outcome. I explained to him how I didn't look at death but life energy as strong or weak. I could see he had only a little over a year until his energy became very low. I could also see change would be difficult for him. I shared only the most optimistic of information believing he could make changes if he decided to. He died in a year and a half.

Likewise, I can sometimes see when the life force energy is high and it does not seem likely death will occur. It doesn't always happen that way but it is a good indicator. When I see a future point of lowered energy, I know that is a critical time and change should be attempted prior to that point.

The man who died of cancer was more focused on medical procedures attempting to save his life, rather than changing any sort of thought patterns. He continued to come for sessions and I continued to see this low energy point in his future.

I read of his death in the paper. It was exactly a year and a half after I first told him his energy would be low at that time. I was very sad he had died, but did not judge the death. I knew he had been comforted by the sessions because he often commented on the tranquility he felt from being there. If that was all that could be done to help his transition, then I was very glad to provide that.

Not everything works out the way we want. I have learned to accept the outcome of my client's healing process. I am not in charge of the world nor of anyone's health. As a health intuitive, I must accept my limitations or otherwise I could not work in a field of life and death circumstances. I learned at the beginning of this not to take on the responsibility of my clients. I can only love them and give them the best sessions I can possibly deliver. I then let go to let them find their own way and their own healing process.

EMERGENCY SITUATIONS

One evening my husband began to experience some chest pains. They were severe enough he was concerned. He asked me to take an intuitive look at the problem. I could see some pulled muscles in the area of the chest. It looked like a recent injury. I could not see any connection to the heart which was his deepest concern. I saw them healing on their own.

After the session, he explained how he had lugged a heavy washer and dryer out of a basement that day. He couldn't use the aid of his cart because of the space limitations on the stairway. He wasn't associating this activity with the pain until after he heard the intuitive session. He then felt certain this was what I was seeing.

In situations of chest pain such as this, I am very concerned about giving someone wrong information. If this had not been my husband, where I was there to monitor the situation, I would have advised him to go to the emergency room. If they need medical treatment, that is what I want for them. I know this process can have errors. I can interpret something wrong, or just be completely off target. Even though I know my accuracy rate is rather high, the percentage of error still exists. This causes me

70

to be very cautious.

I believe health intuitives and physicians can work together. My job as a health intuitive is not to diagnose nor treat anything. One of the areas I stress to my students is to not overstep their boundaries. I always encourage an exam by a qualified practitioner on anything I describe in a session. It is the job of the medical community to diagnose and prescribe. My job is to help you understand yourself from a more wholistic perspective. A health intuitive session is a spiritual session, remember, not physical.

Given my limitations, I never tell anyone to stay away from a doctor. Quite the contrary, I encourage each person to follow their normal health routines. My health intuitive sessions should only complement a complete wellness program.

Occasionally, I have a situation I see as an emergency. I was on the phone setting up an appointment with a woman in California once. Suddenly, I perceived this woman had a severe kidney infection and needed immediate treatment. Because our appointment wasn't for a few days, I mentioned this to her. She was aware of the problem but refused to go to a doctor. I pointed out the dangers involved in not getting help right away. Once again she refused to go to a doctor.

Realizing I wasn't going to have any luck convincing her to go to a doctor, I asked what she knew about natural infection fighting remedies. She had some knowledge of things she could pick up at a health food store. I encouraged her to at least do this much for herself, and if she started feeling any worse, to go to the emergency room right away.

I was concerned for the woman's life as I hung up the phone. I continued to call her throughout the weekend, checking to see if she was okay. She grew weaker and weaker but managed to get a few things at the health food store that may have helped.

Our appointment was scheduled for Monday morning. I was thankful when she called knowing she was still alive. I did the health intuitive session, and when finished, she was convinced she needed some strong antibiotics to fight this infection that had lingered in her body for some time. She made an appointment with a doctor and got the help she needed.

Another evening, I received a call from a good friend, Samantha. I had done several intuitive sessions for her over the years. This night she was suffering from an acute pain in her abdomen and needed help. Normally when someone is suffering with severe pain, I refer them immediately to their doctor. Because I knew Samantha, I decided to take a look and see what the problem was.

I immediately heard the words Milk of Magnesia. I have never purchased this product before in my life. I found it odd I was recommending this to her. Samantha, however, had Milk of Magnesia on hand. Some part of my intuition probably scanned her home and found the thing that would help her the most. I suggested she take some. If she didn't start feeling better, she needed to go to the emergency room. I saw Samantha's problem as gastritis. If I was wrong, the Milk of Magnesia would not fix the problem. I got a call from her in a few hours and her pain was gone.

Sometimes the problem is simple and sometimes we need medical attention. As a health intuitive, I am often called upon to define the difference. The dilemma is deciding if I should do the session. If I decide in an emergency to do a session, I always inform them of the possibility it could be wrong. I never want to harm anyone, but I also do not want to deny the person insight. I always encourage a medical diagnosis. It is the only way we can know for sure if I am right or wrong, and the only ethical way to do the intuitive work I do.

NOT DOCTORS

A health intuitive is not a doctor, a fact both clients and health intuitives forget. A health intuitive is a spiritual counselor. Part of the package is using the physical condition to better understand yourself wholistically. Gaining spiritual understanding is the only reason for describing any sort of the physical condition in a health intuitive session.

Every health intuitive hopes for the best possible physical health for their client. My desire is for the information I provide to be an aid in their overall health and happiness. It is wonderful if it helps them to heal but that isn't the only purpose.

A health intuitive session is not the end to the healing process. Just like the woman with the severe kidney infection, the wholistic information was not going to give her body what it needed. A health intuitive session is informational and helpful, but it does not take the place of a strong antibiotic or emergency surgery when needed.

Health intuitives are not doctors. They can not diagnose anything. When my clients have a pain, they want to know what is physically wrong. That is for their physician to tell them. As a health intuitive, I am to help them understand the spiritual aspects influencing their body.

Chapter Seven

MY HEALING

HEALING CRISIS

Sylvia came to my office for her weekly hypnosis session. She had been dealing with some grief and felt the relaxing technique used in hypnosis helped her. I felt honored she had chosen me as her therapist. She was a physician and knew many psychologists qualified to do this work for her.

One day she asked if I would be interested in participating in a research program in hypnosis. A local institute was starting the project and she was invited to participate. She thought I would be ideal in the program. I was honored to be invited and agreed to participate.

Within a few weeks, Sylvia informed me she was moving to Sweden. She told me to be sure and contact Dr. Choate, the head of the psychology department at the institute doing the hypnosis project. I sent off a letter immediately regarding my interest in their research.

It was 7 a.m. when the call came to my house. I picked up the phone, with curiosity, as to who would be calling at that time of day. It was Dr. Choate. He had my letter in front of him and a few questions for me. First, he wanted to know if I had a doctorate in psychology. After politely informing him I did not, he warned me to be very cautious about practicing hypnosis in the state of Missouri due to a new law making it illegal without a degree.

I was shocked by the call. Could it be my practice was illegal? I started researching the laws and found the term hypnosis had been added to a long list of terms limited to only those licensed to practice psychology. The law was written in such a vague way it was hard to tell just what it meant. It frightened me to think I was doing anything wrong. I decided to stop my practice, at least until I had more answers.

This situation obviously concerned me. I was also concerned about my intuitive work being legal. I always informed my clients of the possibility for error in a session. Still the information bordered on the practice of medicine, law, and psychology. Even though I had never had a single complaint from a client, there was always a first time. I was nervous about proceeding with the work I loved.

I immediately quit my practice and my intuitive work. I even quit teaching the courses. I felt like all I had worked for was now collapsing. I sank into an aimless depressive state without my work motivating me. I was financially sound, so I seldom thought about pursuing a new career. I helped in the real estate management and caught up on reading. Meanwhile, my relationship at the time with my husband was on shaky ground. We just were not close. We had stopped creating together and had little to talk about. The combination of not working and an absent relationship was causing an ill reaction to my health.

This state lasted for about a year. I had very little motivation throughout my day. I grew fatigued. My nervous system became weak. I was very apathetic and listless about my life.

Life force energy grew weak as did my physical condition. My muscles barely carried the weight of my body. I trembled when I was active for any length of time. I was nervous and emotionally could not handle stress. My life was a complete mess.

Finally, my physical condition grew so bad I had to do something. I called for a health intuitive session. I trusted the information would guide me to understand the state I was in and it did.

I realized I needed to improve my relationship and get back to work. I was doing nothing and that was the problem. I sat each day bored and listless. My inner self was trying its best to communicate my desires to me, and yet I ignored this by not responding.

My physical state was very bad, but I already knew that. I had a virus attacking my nervous system. This made me very weak. My muscles and organs were suffering. There was a communication breakdown in my body and in my life. My apathetic attitude was resisting the natural communication occurring in my body. My life was no longer speaking to me nor was I listening.

The intuitive session gave me advice. I first needed to admit there was a communication issue. I had to start tearing down some of these barriers in order for the communication to flow again.

I started with a long talk with my husband. We became more considerate of one another and resolved some of the problems we had been ignoring. Second, I needed to work. I wanted to teach, but felt reluctant to step out and put myself on the line, fearful of the new laws.

I meditated daily to get the answers I needed from within. This helped to establish communication once again between my desires and my actions. My meditations were telling me to work. I needed to use my life energy to help others. I knew this listless apathetic feeling would go away once I let my desires direct my actions. There was no doubt I needed to get my life back on track.

Physically, there were many things that needed to be done. I started a whole healing regimen. Each day I began with meditation followed by a healthy whole grain breakfast. I rested between activities throughout the day. At noon, I did some major fruit and vegetable juicing while sitting in the sun. I let the sunlight filter through my eyelids as I lay back on the deck outside the kitchen. I started acupuncture which helped balance my energy.

My strength began to come back. I could tell a big difference after only a few weeks. I began a daily walking routine and added more fresh vegetables to my diet. I was still very shaky but was returning to a more perfect state of health.

WORKING THE HEALTH INTUITIVE PROGRAM

I studied mind/body relationship books and intuitively did health sessions for myself. I referenced fatigue, the virus I had, and also the nervous and immune systems to try and correlate the message my body was receiving.

In Louise Hay's book *You Can Heal Your Life,* I found the virus I had contracted was a stress related illness. It was caused by having little inner support and not feeling much self-worth. In Dr. Daniel Condron's book *Permanent Healing,* he said the virus came from a mental state of listlessness and feeling little purpose to one's life.

The fatigue, nervous system, and immune system issues were being caused by the virus, but also related with communication and self doubt about creating newness in my life.

I meditated, journaled, and prayed each day for clarity. I was now listening to what my inner self wanted. I took action on my desires, as my body was capable of doing them.

I began to physically feel better and emotionally thrive again. My thoughts were clear and positive. I looked forward to being healthy and vibrant. My life was hopeful even though I was uncertain just where I would go with my work. I overcame many of my fears and began to plan some new activities around the intuitive work I enjoyed so much.

BACK TO WORK

I knew I needed to get back to work and began considering a new course in remote viewing. It was spring and perfect timing to market a class. I began to gather information on how to put the class together. I paced my energy, by working for a time and resting for a time. I continued the juicing, meditating, sun therapy, and acupuncture while working on the class. I worked on all levels of myself as part of my complete healing routine.

I decided on a five day class. I worked diligently to prepare the course. I placed ads in surrounding papers, sent out flyers, and passed out information at conferences. Registrations started to come in. It ended up being one of my largest classes to date.

The class started on a Monday and was to end the following Friday. I was very nervous. It had been a long time since I had taught a class of any sort. This was my first ever remote viewing class. Most of my previous courses were conducted in the evenings which required only a few hours of instruction at a time. This was going to be a five day class from eight in the morning to five in the afternoon each day. This would require some endurance on my part.

I feared I would not have the physical stamina to hold up for the five days. Even though I felt much better than I had a few months earlier, I was still shaky and weak. I calmed my nervous system each morning with meditation. I ate healthy foods and rested often to prepare my body.

I arrived early the first morning with good energy but felt it diminish as the day progressed. My energy was very low by afternoon. I knew I had to make it through five days so I paced myself. I found it difficult to handle any obstacles that came up during the class. My nervous system would react and leave me feeling weak and emotionally stressed. One by one I dealt with the issues at hand. I was totally exhausted at the end of each day, collapsing into bed without a drop of life left in me.

I made it through all five days, but it exhausted me. The class was a great success despite my energy levels being so weak. I had renewed hope. I was a teacher. I would always be a teacher. Even in the face of a healing crises, I was a teacher. I had observed how rich my emotions felt after completing this course. It felt good to work again.

I had taken the efforts needed to reestablish communication both inside my body and in my external life. I realized my need to feel productive and work. My healing continued daily. It took about a year before I felt normal.

I used this experience to understand myself. My body had reflected the state of my soul and spirit. Ignoring my needs didn't make them go away. I had to face my inner desires and take some action on them. Once I did this, my healing immediately began.

The health intuitive session pointed me in all the right directions to start healing. It pointed out all the obstacles I had to overcome. I loved myself enough to take responsibility and do something.

The inner soul and spirit know exactly what is needed. Learning to listen and follow this voice is sometimes hard. It means having to change or do something that may be uncomfortable. You also must admit who you are and your role in healing. No one ever said being responsible was easy, just worth it.

PATTERNS REPEAT

At various points since my healing crisis, I have observed my tendency to be complacent about my life. All I have to do is remember my healing to understand what I must do to be well. I must listen to my inner self. I must figure out a way to take some form of action on the things I want. I must keep a strong line of communication open within. I must have positive communication with those I love.

Keeping these channels of communication and action open keeps me healthier. Since this is a pattern I repeat, this is especially true for me, but is also good advice for anyone.

Everyone has something that gets in their way. For some it is commitment. Others have issues with guilt, control, or fear. All of these things will channel into the body and contribute to the condition of the body. Self-knowledge is key to healing. None of us escape the human factor of emotion, but we can deal with it productively or destructively.

Much of what I teach today is about learning to change destructive patterns into productive ones. I love it when someone becomes empowered by knowing themselves. I have found when people have answers they can make good decisions. Sometimes this translates into healing as it did in my case. For others, they learn how to be happy, successful, or live more true to themselves.

Chapter Eight

LIVING IN HARMONY

UNDERSTANDING RESONANCE

What does it mean to be resonant? We can look at how two waves interact and see a model. When a wave is in resonance with another wave, they amplify each other's wave pattern. When they are not in resonance with one another, they weaken and destroy the wave of the other. This can be demonstrated by viewing the waves made by dropping two pebbles in a pool of water. The waves in resonance will join in the peaks and valleys causing more strength to each wave. Those not in resonance cause a canceling effect of one another and no wave is seen. When two waves move toward one another, they will either resonate and strengthen one another, or not resonate and cancel one another out.

Now imagine your life experiences as a series of energy waves. It is an energy experience of actions and reactions between waves. When you are out of resonance, there is a canceling effect of energy and you feel drained. Remember, the waves around you will resonate and strengthen, or cancel and deplete one another. In order to have a steady, stable flow of energy in your body, you must be in resonance with your life experiences and the wave energy of others.

There are certain people, places, and activities we naturally resonate with. These are the ones we seek out and feel supported by. There is an uplifting feeling associated with them and little effort is needed to harmonize. Likewise, there are certain ways of thinking and feeling which make up our ideals. This is our inner resonance and the substance of our dreams. When we are following these dreams, we are in resonance with our inner self and purpose of our life. Unfortunately, most of life is filled with things we do not easily resonate with.

When I was a child, I enjoyed jumping rope. It was often a common group activity on the playground at the school I attended. Two children would hold the long rope and turn it, while three or four children jumped in rhythm as it passed under their feet.

Once the rope was in motion, it seldom stopped until the end of the play period. The trick was to run into the twirling rope without being tripped and stopping the whole game. We had to find the rhythm of the moving rope and meet that rhythm while moving into the circle. This required harmonizing our speed and body movement with that of the movement of the rope.

Resonating with life is much the same as this early experience of jumping rope. When you recognize that people, organizations, and activities all have a certain resonance or rhythm, you can learn how to harmonize your energy with them. By adapting to the varied resonances of others, you will be able to participate in harmony with all situations. This requires flexibility of attitude and response, but keeps you flowing harmoniously with life. In turn, your life force energy will flow, hopefully keeping you at optimum health.

WHOLISTIC HEALING

A wholistic approach to health involves resonance. It isn't about your body, mind, and spirit operating independent of one another, but rather how well they function together. The foods you eat, air you breathe, and exercise are part of this whole picture. But so is the relationship you have with life and how you feel about yourself.

In Chinese Medicine, life force energy is said to flow through the body giving it vitality. When there is some hindrance to this energy flow, we become susceptible to disease and even accidents. In every experience throughout our day, we have the opportunity to enhance our energy flow or deplete it. This is dependent on how much we are in resonance with our experiences.

When we are in resonance with life, energy naturally flows through the body keeping us healthy. Poor diet, lack of physical activity, emotional upsets, along with mental stress, and failure to experience rest, can cause a lack of resonance in our bodies, and contribute to a slowing down of energy.

Have you ever felt drained of vitality at the end of a day that did not go well? Such a day might start out like a friend of mine's did. She was forced to skip breakfast and an early morning exercise program after her alarm clock failed to go off. She hurried through traffic desperately trying to make an eight o'clock appointment. When she arrived at her office, she was told that her appointment had cancelled the day before. No one had bothered to inform her of this, however. She was emotionally upset with her staff and terribly disappointed about the client's cancellation. She worried about the reason her client had cancelled. Her sales had been down the past few months, and she feared her job might be on the line. This was an important account and one she couldn't afford to lose. Her body tensed as she became more and more concerned.

As the day progressed, nothing seemed to go well for her. Little things became irritants, like the line at the gas station, and the music playing on the radio. The more she focused on her problems, the unhappier she became. As her dissatisfaction grew stronger, she was more and more irritated.

By the time she arrived home, she was exhausted with a splitting headache. Everyone wanted her attention, but she was just too tired to give it. She wanted to avoid talking to anyone and excused herself from the family shared dinner by going to bed early. Trying to force herself to sleep didn't work either. She tossed and turned until she gave up and got out of bed. She watched television only to become bored and turned to reading a book. The book didn't hold her interest so she just sat, staring at the wall, exhausted and unhappy.

I think it would be safe to say my friend was out of resonance with her life that day. Her body and mind were not in harmony with her experiences. She responded with ill emotions and physical distress. She was tense, irritable, and in pain. Her energy depleted, along with her joy of living, as the day went by. If every day were like this, her body would soon be jeopardized of good health.

Resonance is created when we are harmonizing with life's situations. When you find yourself in a disagreeable circumstance, find some common ground, something you like, or at least something you can tolerate about it. This will bring resonance with your environment and your energy will not be depleted.

How many people do you know that spend much of their life stressed? They are unhappy, driven, and pushing the limits of their energy reserve. Rejuvenating the body and mind are not built into their daily routines. They are out of resonance with their life experience, and look to the circumstances of their life to blame, rather than to harmonize with what is present.

RECOGNIZING RESONANCE

When you are in resonance with your life, you will be in harmony, enhancing the energy flow of your body, mind, and spirit. Emotions are harmony monitors. They keep us informed as to how well we are resonating with life. Emotionally, we feel good when we resonate with our life experiences, and out of sync when we do not.

Life force energy has no judgments attached. It is just energy like the wind that turns the windmill, like the fuel that makes your car go down the road, and like the water that creates electricity. It is the human element of perception that attaches judgments. We respond in positive and negative ways depending on how satisfied we are with a situation. This response plays a role in resonance causing us to have enhanced or hindered energy.

Resistance creates a failure to resonate. When you are going against the flow of any situation, it automatically depletes your energy. This doesn't mean you should go along with every situation, only that to live in constant resistance is to live a life out of resonance. Eventually, this will cause an energy depletion in your body and possibly illness. Harmony restores energy and good health.

Resonance is important in every part of your day. Harmonizing with your body as it digests food, exercises, and rests, gives you more vitality. We live in a society that often hurries through meals, giving little attention to the process of digestion. Being of a fast food culture, we eat quickly knowing little about how the food affects our bodies. When was the last time you asked yourself if you were in resonance with your lunch? Is the food healthy? Is it what your body needs? Do you even enjoy the taste or has it become a habit to eat what is easy? The same is true of exercise and relaxation.

Mindfulness is required to be in resonance. Do a double check periodically to know if you are in harmony with your experiences. If you feel a sense of dissatisfaction, you have choices. Either change your activity to one you are in harmony with, or adjust your attitude to be in harmony with your circumstance.

Since we are all, at times, in situations where we have no or little choice to change our activity, it is important to learn how to adjust our thoughts and emotions to create resonance. This is not a process of control, but rather a simple procedure involving acknowledgment and flow of energy.

When I first started my self-awareness search, I read many books about how to be happy. By turning all negative thoughts into positive ones, I would be able to only experience the happy, bright side of life. Road blocks were set up throughout my system prohibiting a single thought that might even hint of negativity.

After trying this for a few years, I began to notice how lifeless I felt. I was really out of harmony with my enjoyment of living. This was the opposite of what I was attempting to achieve. I discovered I had been repressing a very natural flow of energy in my body by being in denial of all emotions that didn't make me feel good. By not blocking these feelings but acknowledging them, I could let them go very quickly and once again gain harmony.

MAKE CHOICES THAT RESONATE WITH YOU

It is important to recognize who you are and place yourself

with people, in organizations, and work places that resonate best with your personal ideals. This creates optimum energy and resonance for your life.

Resonance in your relationships, career choice, and recreational activities, are equally significant as are harmonizing with your needs, desires, and dreams. These areas of life are more under your control and should be wisely considered.

We are often influenced by expectations of others, society's rules, and our own lack of self-awareness, leading us down paths that are dissatisfying. We may even make good decisions only to outgrow them with time. Don't be afraid to make changes when you find you are not in resonance. By creating the most harmonious atmosphere in your environment, you will be enabling your body to increase and balance energy flow.

Don't get caught up in the trap of feeling guilty for making changes, or being pressured to conform to what others want of you. Let your inner thoughts and feelings guide your decisions, and monitor how you resonate with your choices.

MIND/BODY RELATIONSHIP

When disease occurs, there is a war going on. A war between forces that move energy and forces that keep it stagnant. When we try to stop life from progressing in a naturally flowing way, it is like building a dam. Life force energy is always trying to move through the body. When it encounters a blocked area, prohibiting it to flow, you may experience pain, irritation, or disease in that area.

Because perception is a strong director of life force energy, our thoughts and feelings play a big role in the way energy flows in the body. Certain ways of thinking and feeling communicate very specific messages. When we think and feel a certain way, the body reacts causing a chain of events that may result in disease.

Thoughts and feelings transfer to specific areas of the body. Many of these you may be familiar with and others may not be as obvious. Much of our language reflects this correlation between thoughts and areas of the body. When we find someone irritating, we may refer to them as being a pain in the neck. When we are anxious, we notice butterflies in the stomach. We have a broken heart when a love goes wrong and our shoulders feel it when we are on overload, or have too much responsibility.

Less obvious thought to body reactions are things like guilt channeling to the kidneys, power issues influencing the pancreas, and the throat being affected by our lack of willingness to say what is on our minds.

Every thought moves energy in your body, be it small or large. It is important to let hindering thoughts and feelings pass quickly and replace them with something constructive. In other words, as soon as you recognize someone is irritating, forgive the thought and avoid a stiff neck. When you are anxious about something, relax, and let that upset stomach pass. And finally, speak up and turn a tendency toward laryngitis away.

Most major diseases come from a strong attitude that depletes the system. These attitudes have been charted among those suffering from certain disorders. A short list of diseases and their thought bases follows. Keep in mind these are general, not specific.

Cancer: Deep hurt, long standing resentments.
Heart Attack: Competitive attitude, feeling life is difficult in regards to love, money, and security.
Arthritis: Feeling restricted and unloved. Critical attitude.

Diabetes: Thinking of what might have been rather than working with what is. Refusing to give from what exists and stepping into your own power.

Stroke: Refusing to face life.

Colds: Indecision, confusion.

Back Problems: Not feeling supported in life. Inflexible.

Parkinson's Disease: Withdrawal. Wanting more control over your personal circumstances.

Overweight: Self-protection, wanting more from life, insecure.

Many of these personality traits have been pointed out in mainstream studies. We have all heard of the type A personality and their susceptibility to heart disease. Even though the type A personality has been recognized, many others have not. You may read more about the mind/body relationship in *You Can Heal Your Life* by Louise Hay and *Permanent Healing* by Daniel Condron.

I once knew a girl who was having difficulty with her roommate. She would often call me up complaining about the intolerable conditions she was forced to live under. No matter how much she tried to reason with her roommate, nothing changed. She didn't feel she could afford to move and so felt trapped.

After a few months of feeling this way, my friend was rushed to the emergency room with an appendicitis attack. When I looked up the mind/body relationship, it clearly pointed out the state of mind she had been experiencing. One of the thought patterns associated with this disorder, was repressing a dissatisfaction with your environment, causing an explosion in your body.

Our bodies do respond in very certain ways to a thought or feeling. This was clearly shown to me years ago when, on two separate occasions, I came down with a severe cold. Both times

I was in a quandary about making a trip during adverse winter road conditions. My fear of driving on icy roads was causing me to vacillate on whether or not to go at all. Each time I would decide to go, I changed my mind, only to finally decide at the last minute to take the trip. Both times I returned with a terrible cold.

Colds are generated from the thought pattern of indecisiveness. From that point to now, I have become aware when I am being indecisive and have avoided colds for years by directing my thoughts.

A HEALTH INTUITIVE SESSION

I was teaching my health intuitive process at a conference when a man asked if healing was caused through doing one of these sessions. I explained how the session itself didn't heal. It was taking the information and applying it to make the inner changes in thoughts and emotions that could assist someone to heal.

Learning how to resonate your personal wave with life around you promotes harmony and harmony promotes healing. When the war between stagnation and growth ceases, the body can then begin the healing process. Thoughts and emotions are but one part of this process, but certainly contribute to the way the energy is enhanced or depleted.

You can adjust your thoughts and feelings to resonate with almost any given environment. When you know your resonate wave, you can choose to live life surrounded by resonate waves that assist and strengthen your own. The health intuitive session is a means to help you know your self, and how well you are harmonizing with your life.

Chapter Nine

UNSEEN CONNECTIONS

INTUITIVE BROADCASTING

The more I have become involved with intuition, the clearer it is to me we are built with a sending/receiving ability on a mental level. Communication is occurring all the time even when we are unaware. We have meaningful and influential impact on one another at a thought level beneath the surface of our conscious awareness. Having a thought of someone automatically connects us with them and vice versa. Most of this goes unnoticed. and has only minor impact on the outcome of events in our lives.

I like to think of intuition as a broadcasting network. When I have positive uplifting thoughts about something, that is what I am broadcasting to that person or event. When I have a negative, discouraging thought, then that is what I am broadcasting. How much impact this may have on someone depends on how sensitive they are to the broadcast. Generally relatives and close friends are most aware of one another's thoughts. This explains how families often know when another family member is in trouble, or how you know when a friend needs a call. It is because the two of you have close mental and emotional ties. This puts you on a similar broadcasting frequency.

I once spoke with a woman whose brother passed away in a foreign country. At the time of his death, she was on a camping trip with her family and small dog. While her brother suffered a painful death on the other side of the world due to eating poisonous fish, her dog began to take on some very strange symptoms. Fearful he had been bitten by a snake, she rushed him to a nearby town to see a vet. They could not find a cause for the small dog's intense condition. She took the small animal back to the camp and sat awake with him all night.

The next morning the dog's symptoms had completely disappeared. He awoke bright and cheery seeming perfectly fine. Soon they received the tragic news of her brother's death. Once they knew the cause, they researched the progression of symptoms he must have suffered. They were identical to the symptoms the dog had exhibited the night before.

She had always been very close to her brother and believed he was trying to get in touch with her through her dog. She was convinced her attentiveness to the dog through the night somehow reached her brother around the world, where he too felt her comforting love, as he made his transition out of this world.

EVERY THOUGHT MAKES A CONNECTION

Our thoughts may broadcast further than just friends and relatives, however. Research done by Dr. Lloyd, Dr. Justa Smith, and Dr. Douglas Dean, has demonstrated how the subconscious or autonomic system of the body responds to intuitive signals. There was a point in my intuitive development when I realized this was vital to understand. There are social responsibilities involved in what we think, for it is sending a subtle broadcast.

If it is socially unacceptable to be rude to another person in a conversation, then it is unacceptable to be rude to another person in our thoughts. Aggressive thought patterns, selfishness, demands of others, are influential thoughts. If it is unacceptable to be a bully face to face, then it should be unacceptable to be a bully to someone in our thoughts.

Playing fair takes on a whole new meaning when we enter the world of intuition. It has been shown in studies of sending and receiving intuitive signals that the autonomic system of the body responds. If I have a negative thought projected toward you, it may actually cause your immune system to lower its effectiveness. Likewise, if it is a loving and positive thought, your immune system may slightly improve. If we are responsible with our thoughts they will be loving.

If I am able to broadcast my thoughts in such a way as to harm you, then it is the same as physically abusing you. In many ways, I have consciously slapped you in the face or in this case, the autonomic system.

Taking responsibility for our thoughts is as important as taking responsibility for our actions. Most of us would not go out and rob a bank, beat up a neighbor, or yell in the face of a co-worker. We are socially conditioned not to do these things and take the social responsibility to be good citizens and neighbors. But do we stop ourselves from having harmful thoughts? There is no social structure which makes us aware of the harm or damage we may be causing.

Thoughts and emotions are the channels humans use to project intuition. We get angry at family, friends, and neighbors, and project unkind thoughts. These can be very destructive. When someone doesn't do what we want them to do, we may think unfavorably about them. When was the last time you were at a check out stand and felt upset with the clerk because they took too much time? Did you have unkind thoughts toward them? When was the last time you were late for an appointment

I decided to intuitively connect with my husband and start an intuitive conversation with him. He was busy as I knew he would be. He was able to compromise his busy schedule though, and told me he would be there by 10:47. I had a bit of a wait but I occupied my time well. At exactly 10:47, he pulled in the driveway surprised I was there.

He had no idea we had had an intuitive conversation earlier that day. I was talking with his subconscious, and was fully aware of it, but he had no idea. He acted on my request to come to the house and unlock the door, and even created a reason.

I am not the only one doing this, but most people do it without awareness. My students are able to send and receive messages with one another which we have documented. I have to believe, if I am doing this and my students are doing this, then we are all doing this.

The moral question lies in how much we are influencing someone's free will. Once I became aware of the impact of my thoughts, I became far more considerate of the way I think.

I fear we are all guilty of causing others to think in ways that are not of their choice. A dominant thought projected to another can enter their mind and be conceived as their own. Some people are so strong and dominant in their thoughts, they are what I call inner level bullies. These people go around influencing others to succumb to their will, with absolutely no regard for the free will choice of other people.

Parents are often guilty of this with their children. They want a certain behavior and response from the child. To a point this works when they are young, but after a time, it is good for the child to learn to recognize their own thoughts separate from their parents.

With or without awareness, this borders on controlling another person. Mind control sounds so abusive and interfering, and yet it can happen on a totally innocent scale, when one is not aware of the power of their own thoughts.

I once heard a lady talk about using her mind to restructure her work place. She had a supervisor that she did not like and felt was inefficient at her job. She felt another person in the office would be much better in this position. She began to project to the unwanted supervisor that she would become unhappy in her position and start looking for work elsewhere. At the same time, she started projecting thoughts to the owners of the business, to place the woman she liked in the supervisor position. Within a few months, all of this transpired.

Did they act on their free will, or was it her projection that caused this change? That is a difficult question to answer, but knowing what I do today, I would have to say her thoughts had an impact. Much needs to be learned about the way our thoughts are connected and how we influence one another.

RESPONSIBLE USE OF THOUGHT

We have a concept that we are each self-contained in our own unique little world of thought. That somehow, my thoughts and your thoughts, are in no way related. Yet studies show this is not true. When someone is thinking of you, your brain waves and body chemistry respond. On some subconscious level, you are aware of the thought of another. This can influence your thinking. At the same time, your thoughts are influencing others. Taking responsibility and understanding this may be the next stage in human development.

I had been working with my intuition for some time, when one day it came to me in meditation, to be aware of inner level etiquette. This was certainly a new term and I wasn't sure what it even meant. I explored the possibilities. Socially, we are taught to interact with one another in respectful ways. This keeps society running and lets us all get along. No one teaches us how to think with etiquette. Most believe their thoughts are hidden and there are no manners needed.

If you have ever been in the presence of someone who just makes you feel good, most likely you are picking up on the kinds of thoughts they are having. At the same time, I am certain you have been in the presence of people who make you feel uncomfortable. Perhaps these are people who are projecting some ill feelings. Their outer social demeanor may fit the social rules, but their thoughts may be stepping over that boundary.

On an even more subtle level, you may be influenced by people not even in your presence. If that person is thinking of you, it will draw the attention of your subconscious mind. Your conscious mind may never be aware of this directly, but subconsciously you are responding. Likewise, you may be doing the same with others. My clients are often surprised I can do an intuitive session with them even when they are halfway around the world. This is because thought is not contained in the body, but is like a broadcasting wave. Distance is irrelevant.

Learning inner level etiquette is a new idea. It requires awareness of thought, not just interaction. There is a new level of responsibility with this, but also a new freedom. Remember, others may have impolite thoughts directed toward you. If you don't want to be mistreated and wish to think for yourself, then you must become aware of this communication on an intuitive level.

New social standards must be learned for inner level etiquette to begin. These are not standards that dictate behavior, but rather thinking. The real process for human change may come from awareness of thought rather than action. The possibility for world peace, a loving society, and finding the secret to personal fulfillment, may be found in this discovery.

POSITIVE BROADCASTING

The moral issue with intuitive broadcasting is how it is used. It is wise to use it as a means to make life better rather than to be invasive and harmful. Things like world peace, healing, and to reduce crime are a few ways this has been done.

Thought is the most intimate part of ourselves. We can project our thoughts and emotions in a thoughtful way or be invasive. To deliberately invade the space of a person's thinking for the purpose of gathering information about them without permission is morally wrong. If you would not rape a person's body, then why would you invade the privacy of their thoughts? This is about respect. So many intuitives are out to impress others with their abilities. They are ego driven and so the idea of invasion never enters their mind. Even the best intended intuitive may cross the boundaries of another person's personal space without intending to do so. Without permission you are forcing yourself on another, and to me this is a kind of rape of the mind. You wouldn't walk into someone's home uninvited, so why walk into their mind.

Love is always an appropriate broadcast and will influence most any situation for good. When our general thoughts and emotions are in a loving state they naturally increase the amount of love we will experience in our lives. When we broadcast in a more specific way healing influence, changing lives, and the positive outcome of events can be influenced.

Chapter Ten

WHERE DID THIS FEELING COME FROM?

UNADDRESSED ABUSES

Intuition can be intrusive when it is used without awareness. I had been working with my intuitive skills for several years before I realized just how influential intuition could be. It was an ordinary day. I was alone, working around the house, when suddenly I started having argumentative thoughts about a fellow researcher. I had no reason to be arguing with Larry, the researcher, which confused me. We had our differences, but there was no logic behind my sudden angry thoughts.

As the day went on, I continued to think about Larry in controversial ways. I tried to ignore the thoughts, but they popped right back. Periodically I examined them. I was very upset with him but for the life of me, I could not figure out why. The feelings persisted with no logic to them. I had to ignore them in order to finish my work.

Later that evening, I received a telephone call from Sal, another researcher. Sal, Larry and I were the leading researchers of the paranormal in our area. Larry and I conducted monthly meetings heading separate organizations. Sal often attended these meetings. Occasionally, we all shared research information with one another.

When Sal called, he began by stating he had been thinking about calling me all day. He wanted to run something by me to see what I thought. For the next twelve minutes, he did nothing but complain about Larry. He was very upset and was uncertain what to do. Larry had taken some of Sal's research and claimed it as his own. Sal wanted my opinion regarding this action. Should he call Larry and explain how he felt? Should he just ignore the situation? Was he justified in his feelings? It was obvious he was in conflict. I realized, I too, had been in conflict about this situation all day, even though I didn't know why until now.

After my conversation with Sal, I came to understand the feelings I had struggled with that day. Intuitively, I was aware of the situation between Sal and Larry. With the call from Sal, it all made sense. Sal's thoughts of me drew my awareness into the midst of their controversy. I was siding with Sal causing the argumentative feelings in me toward Larry. I was aware just enough to realize my feelings. Had I explored it further, I could have become more aware of the whole picture.

The importance of this incident, for me, was to understand how much our thoughts are in communication with one another all the time. We may assume our minds are independent, but there are exchanges happening between us we may be unaware of. Our thoughts are not isolated. They are very connected to one another, and may be influential to the way we think and feel.

I gave an example, in an earlier chapter, of my friend looking at her watch just as I was thinking about her arrival time for dinner. This is another prime example. Our thoughts are very connected on an intuitive level. When we think about a person, it is like dialing them up on the phone, only it is a frequency, rather than a number that connects us. When Sal thought about calling me, it automatically connected me with his thoughts. I responded even though I was unaware he was thinking of me.

Our thoughts are not totally independent, that is the point I am trying to make here.

Follow me for a moment with the possibilities here. If we are able to call each other up by just thinking about one another, and we respond to these thoughts, then we are influencing one another in some way. There are whole schools out there teaching this very thing called remote influencing. This kind of influence can be for good or it can be misused. It will depend on the moral character of the one doing the remote influencing.

We have very specific rules of social conduct and even laws protecting the mistreatment of one person to another. I certainly would not walk up to a stranger and hit him. For one thing he might hit me back, and second, I could be arrested on assault charges. Yet intuitively, I can think every bad thought I want about him. I can dislike the way he looks, the way he walks, and the way he talks. I can throw an angry thought to the person who cuts me off in traffic, or a friend who does not return my telephone call.

If these thoughts and feelings were transferred to physical gestures, they might be pushes, shoves, or slaps. If it is a really upsetting thought, it could equate to a severe blow. Intense thought registers in the receiver's subconscious mind. The subconscious responds to both loving, caring thoughts, as well as hateful destructive thoughts.

There are no social rules in place regarding thoughts. Many great spiritual teachers of the world knew the effects of thought, and taught this in their teachings. This is presented to help us understand that thinking something is the same as doing it. We are not a society that takes much responsibility for the way we think. We have long promoted the idea of the individual and separation, without understanding our connectedness.

TO THE EXTREME

In a few extreme forms of remote influencing, death occurs. It has been reported that the Huna Shamans, native to the Hawaiian Islands, could project the thought of death to a menacing figure and take their life. This was done each year, and the results were always the same. First the person experienced paralysis, then the organs began to shut down, and finally death. It was a ritualistic event intended to rid the island of any bad apples among them.

Remote influencing can be used with very negative results, possibly even death. If we look at the same type of influence for good, we might see the work of healers. Healers most often work through prayer. Major research is being done on this powerful force on the body to heal. The point being, that powerful minds are able to influence others in dramatic ways.

VALUE OF INTUITIVE COMMUNICATION

We influence one another in very subtle ways every day through our thoughts. We may influence someone's immune system, either positively or negatively, depending on the thought we project. Projecting confidence in someone may actually increase their self-esteem. How often have you seen a student excel because a teacher believes in them, or a coach set an expectation for the players of a team, helping them to meet that expectation?

I tried this once with a remote viewing class. I had just started a radio show at the time. A show was scheduled on remote viewing with some of the students of this class appearing as guests. I needed this class to do very well. Nothing could be worse than a bunch of students saying aloud on public radio how hard it is to learn remote viewing.

I decided to do some remote influencing before the class began. I connected intuitively with the minds of each student a few days before the class started. Step by step, I led them through the remote viewing process, telling them exactly how I wanted each to perform.

This was all done intuitively, mind to mind, before I even met the students. I mentally negotiated with each one, asking them to do their best. I gave them remote mental demonstrations on how to get to the information. I didn't know the targets, so I was not feeding them answers in advance, only the process of remote viewing.

There were five students in the class. A retired man and his wife who were in their seventies. Neither had any experience in remote viewing, nor did they feel they had any intuitive abilities. There were two women, one a medical doctor, and the other a medical technician. Both had limited intuitive experiences, but nothing they could depend on to be accurate. The third student was a man with extensive remote viewing training. He had taken several well known courses in remote viewing from some of the top trainers in the country. The class was a real mix of intuitive skill.

Ned was the skilled remote viewer. I was curious that he wanted to take this course since he was already trained in remote viewing. It became evident after talking with Ned, why it was important he revisit the classroom of remote viewing.

It seems Ned had initially trained himself to remote view from instructions in a book. Then he proceeded to take the courses, but found the process cumbersome. Even though he could do it, the manner was discouraging. He almost completely lost the skill after taking the courses. He wanted to do remote viewing again, and thought my method might be the thing to bring his skill back.

Ned's remote viewing sessions were very accurate from the beginning. By the end of four days, the whole group was doing very well. The retired woman, who started out unable to remote view anything, ended the course by immediately knowing her blind target. It was the most accurate remote viewing class I ever taught. I couldn't help but believe it had something to do with the remote influencing I did prior to the start of the class.

Remote influencing can improve most anything we do. You must remember to respect those involved and request their participation. If I simply told them what to do then I would be taking advantage of their minds. It would no longer be fair but abusive. That is the moral stand we all must address with this skill. Without a framework of ethics, we are just selfishly trying to control others.

The remote viewing class notably improved with remote influencing. I have done this in other situations and the response is the same.

UNSUSPECTING INFLUENCE

Many years ago, I spent my days working at home. My husband would often come home for lunch. I would be going about my day in peace when he arrived. Sometimes we talked, and other times we would just quickly eat a bite, and go back to work.

I noticed on some days, a real change in my feelings after lunch time. I would sometimes feel frustrated or angry. After awhile, I began to understand what was happening. If my husband was having an especially disturbing day at work, even though he didn't verbally express it, I was intuitively receptive to his feelings.

Once I became aware of this problem, I could be

objective, understanding they were not my feelings, but his. I was able to separate them from me knowing they did not generate from my own experiences. When you are highly intuitive, you may become consciously aware of another's feelings. A person who is not highly intuitive may be influenced at a subconscious level, but not feel the emotions of the other person. Either way, we are influenced to some degree.

My intuition seems to work like radar when people are having some difficulties in life. My friend's sister, whom I had never met, came to me in a dream one night very distressed. I called my friend the next day only to find out her sister had been going through a very difficult situation. I was driving down the road one day when I suddenly knew an elderly relative was in some physical distress. Later that week, he was diagnosed with a very debilitating disorder they had not suspected before. A man I worked with many years before was having some serious financial problems, and it was made clear to me he needed help.

Chapter Eleven

ALL FOR ONE AND ONE FOR ALL

WE ARE NOT ISOLATED IN A MENTAL VACUUM

The idea of a collective consciousness has been with us since Carl Jung introduced the idea. Science is not able to explain how this can be, but looking at the vast amount of research done on the matter, it is difficult to deny it is true. Some of the most documented scientific studies, showing how interconnected our minds are, were done at Stanford Research Institute and the Princeton Engineering Anomalies Research labs.

At Stanford, Russell Targ and Harold Puthoff discovered, through a number of experiments, the ability of minds to intuitively perceive. Through intuition alone, a person could see where another person was, what they were doing, and even know what they were thinking. As part of one experiment, they sent someone out of the lab to an unknown destination. A viewer in the lab, using only their mental ability, would describe the other person's surroundings. They found this could be done consistently, could be learned with a structured program, and with practice the viewer improved.

Anyone with normal intelligence was capable of learning this. From the research, one can not help but believe this is a widespread latent ability residing in, possibly, a collective consciousness.

Princeton Engineering Anomalies Research lab, at Princeton University, was able to duplicate the same findings as Stanford. They were even able to do this as far away as Paris with the same results. They found distance to have no effect on the accuracy or strength of the viewer to receive the correct information.

In my research, I have found the exact same results. I have practiced this in many ways, but in one class I had a person go to a small shopping center with a little courtyard and fountain outside. One by one, I had my students view the scene through the eyes of the one at the shopping center. The students had no idea where the person was located. Then I asked them to find one object at this location that would verify they were looking at the same location as the distant person.

One man began to describe a fountain. He could see it clearly and captured the sound of the water, the three tiers, and saw it in the middle of an outside area that was well groomed. He even saw the ornate design on the fountain.

Another woman, viewing the same location, heard a musical sound like bells. They didn't sound all the time, but when they did, they created a nice variety of tones. The sound was located near a white painted wooden door with glass panels.

After the remote viewing sessions, we drove to the location of the distant person. The students explored what they had been remotely seeing. They found everything as they had seen in their minds earlier. The fountain was in the middle of the courtyard, and the wind chimes hung by a shop door.

In another experiment, I had each student think of some event from their past. I asked them to have the memory clear in their minds before pairing up with another student. Once with a partner, they were to determine which one would send and which one would receive. Then the sender would think about the event from their past, and the receiver would describe what they saw. When finished, they switched roles. Six out of seven students described the scenes with accurate detail. In many cases, they were able to get details, like the age of the person, their emotional state, and the activity that was taking place at the event.

LINKING UP

Mind to mind communication is provable in controlled scientific experiments, showing our consciousness is not isolated in a vacuum, as we are led to believe. There is supporting evidence done through research on brain waves. Use of an EEG shows when two minds become synchronized with one another, their brain wave patterns match.

In *The High Performance Mind*, Anna Wise shows how a mother's brain waves shift when she is nursing and feeling especially connected with her baby. Her brain waves will have an almost identical pattern as the child's. When she is not nursing or interacting with the baby, they go back to her normal pattern. In other cases, they have shown two people in a compatible relationship will often exhibit like brain wave patterns. They have even been able to show that a horse and rider may become synchronized, exhibiting similar brain waves. This shows a connection between minds that goes far beyond what we can see.

In one case, horseback riding was being used as a therapy for disabled children. When the child was placed on a horse with a disorganized brain wave pattern, the child's brain waves also became disorganized. When the same child was placed on a horse with well organized brain waves, his also became organized. There was obviously a connection occurring between the animal and child.

FREQUENCY

We are each born with a signature brain wave pattern giving us our mental identity much like DNA or fingerprints. These patterns have a rhythm that shift in varied situations. An empathetic personality is able to easily shift their pattern to match another's. This will make the two feel compatible and connected.

Some people are more flexible than others in shifting their brain waves to match another person's. Those who are more fixed in their brain wave patterns may be somewhat insensitive, and far less empathetic, incapable of placing themselves in another person's shoes or mind so to speak. Those who are flexible with their mind, and unafraid of stepping out of their personal brain wave signature, are very good at connecting with others. They will be more sensitive, empathetic, and compatible personalities.

With training and feedback, anyone can learn how to synchronize their brain wave patterns to match another person's. One can even expand beyond an individual and connect with a group mentality. Imagine expanding to a point inclusive of the collective consciousness, or even beyond, to be synchronized with the universe.

Chapter Twelve

Logic Vs intuition

DUALITY OF INTELLIGENCE

When I was nineteen, I dated a man who was a psychologist. We were riding around the countryside in his convertible sports car one Sunday afternoon, enjoying the sun, when I noticed some cows grazing in a pasture. I made a remark about animal instinct, and he came back with the absolute statement that instinct is a characteristic of animals that people do not possess.

Animals were somehow given this radar device that humans simply were not endowed with. They just know the who, what, where, and how of survival where humans must figure it out. Of course, this gives humans more freedom to create new ways to survive, rather than just operating off a subconscious program.

Humans have a far more complex system to help them make their way through life. When we take a look at the human brain, we can see how it divides into many parts, but we will talk about only four, the left and right hemispheres, and the frontal and hind brain. The left and right hemispheres of the brain work together, but contribute in different ways. The left is concerned with logic, while the right side has the big picture in mind, and is more intuitive. The frontal lobe is the executive center of the brain, and involves comprehension and short term memory. While the frontal lobe is taking care of matters at hand, the hind brain is steadily keeping you alive by controlling all of your vital bodily functions. This is done through the autonomic system of the body.

Thank goodness we have the hind brain, for without it, we would spend all our time running the body. Imagine needing to tell yourself to breathe, circulate your blood, and digest your food. It would be the only thing you would accomplish.

We are going to simplify how these four parts work together. The frontal lobe and left hemisphere we will call our logical intelligence. The hind brain and the right hemisphere we will call intuitive intelligence. This creates a duality between the logical and intuitive parts of the brain. Even though all parts of the brain work together at all times, we will refer to these as separate working divisions, in order to make our point of duality.

LOGICAL INTELLIGENCE

Because we use a bit more of the left and frontal portions of the brain during our waking and working states, we have come to give them priority. We base many exams of intelligence on how well the left and frontal parts of the brain function, which we call logic.

These are the areas we like to see develop in children, assuming if they have logic and reasoning, they will do well in life. These parts of the brain are aggressive thinking centers, and so the more aggressive the thinker, the more progressive the results. We have created major programs to encourage the active use of our logical intelligence. This includes reading, doing well on exams, and analytically making decisions.

Logical intelligence likes everything to be neat and complete. Everything has a correct answer and one and one always add up to two. If it doesn't add up, then our logic doesn't really like to deal with it. It moves on to the next problem that does not contain any ambiguity about it. Thus life runs smoothly and we have all the answers.

We have grown to trust, and sort of worship, this logical intelligence. This attitude has created a number of biases regarding intelligence itself. What is thought to be intelligence is always logical, reasonable, and consistent. It requires work to attain, is exact, and proves our reality. It is always direct, focused, and analytical in nature. And finally, this form of intelligence is mature and adult like. Therefore, most problem solving and decision making are based on logical thinking.

INTUITIVE INTELLIGENCE

The other half of intelligence is intuitive rather than logical. It is a far more subtle kind of intelligence and therefore less obvious. In contrast to the more black and white views of its counterpart, it is creative, imaginative, and innovative.

Intuitive intelligence breaks all the rules of how we are taught to think. Even in the face of all the logic and reason in the world, it may disagree. The reason for this is, because it is looking at the big picture and taking into account many things that are not addressed in statistical reports and data analysis.

Where logic does well on exams, intuition performs best in real life situations. It is that knowing in the moment if something will or will not work. There is nothing to back it up, no logic behind it, just a feeling. It is that hunch, that gut feeling, or snap decision made just because you know it is right. At a more advanced state, it becomes our intuition guiding us to successful living.

Intuitive intelligence has been shown to be as valuable in life situations, as logic is in learning and retaining knowledge. In emergency rooms across the country, physicians must depend on their intuition to make lifesaving decisions on the spot. These are unpredictable situations that can not afford long thought-out moments of reasoning. The right action must be taken in many cases very quickly. Without the ability of intuitive intelligence to immediately address the big picture and act, the patient could die. At that moment, the physician must rely on good intuitive judgment. It is the make or break of a good ER doctor. I often work with medical professionals, helping them to develop their intuitive intelligence, to complement the logical knowledge they have already attained.

Another area where intuition will supercede logic is in timing. Timing is an important factor to successful living. It is our intuitive intelligence that keeps track of timing. Seeing the global big picture, it is always feeding us with information. Having been a real estate investor for years, I have noticed the value of timing for successful investing. Any high risk speculation can pay off or in some cases take you financially under. It is not a place where you can afford to make many bad decisions. Those who are most successful will admit to having a good sense of timing with an investment. That sense of timing is a feeling coming from their intuition.

There are people who are good at what they do and then there are leaders. Research shows that it is not the person with the highest scores or the ones who have followed all the logical rules that are most successful. It is that person who understands how the big picture and little picture fit together that succeeds. They have a good grip on both logic and intuition.

When creativity drops, you know you are out of touch with your intuition, because intuition is always innovative by nature. When we are not using the intuitive intelligence we were born with, we may feel like we are living in a box. This stagnant feeling contributes to even less creativity. Everyone seems to be in this box, so it seems foolish to even think about stepping out of it. The continued lack of use of your intuition guarantees you will stay locked and unaware. The beginning point of using both sides of intelligence is to accept that intuition is real.

Since we are programmed to believe playful ideas have little value, after all they are not mature, we tend to ignore them. Yet innovative and intuitive thinking encourages finding healthy solutions in unconventional ways. The broad-mindedness of the intuitive side of intelligence opens possibilities we may never think of otherwise. These ideas do not come through hard analytical thinking. They are subtle intuitive impressions.

Not wanting to deal with errors, ambiguity, and society's opinions, keeps us tightly clinging to the standards we have been taught, and using only half of our intelligent capacity. It is impossible to develop a well rounded person without learning how to balance hard and soft thinking together. Hard thinking being logical, soft thinking being intuitive.

Decision making, from logic alone, limits us to creating life from what is known. This leaves little room for new ideas and new learning to occur. Doing something that doesn't work well the first time will most likely not work well when repeated. The big picture, from intuitive intelligence, is needed to see the broad scope of the unknown. At an intuitive glance, a better method, a new way of thinking, a change in perspective, may offer great advantages.

Major breakthroughs in business, and even in personal living, often come by unconventional means. An answer will come out of the blue after waking from a dream, in the middle of watching a movie, or relaxing with a cup of tea. That is how intuition communicates, in those relaxed subtle moments of living, where there is suddenly insight. Insight that can not, will not, does not, communicate while we have our thoughts busy trying to come up with an answer. That is because the intuitive intelligence comes to us when we are in a receptive state of mind. When our thoughts are quiet, we can then sense intuitively.

Chapter Thirteen

BENDING THE MIND

FLEXIBLE CONSCIOUSNESS

I was working on a course a few years ago to help people gain greater states of awareness. As I intuitively looked at the course material, I realized what I was teaching was how to have a flexible mind. Physically we become more flexible through stretching the muscles of the body. Mentally we become more flexible by moving and stretching the many states of consciousness available to us.

A flexible mind, as I am referring to it, does not just mean an open mind, even though that might accompany the process. The type of flexibility I am speaking of is one where our state of consciousness can easily shift. One where we are able to move in and out of various states of consciousness with great precision. The four basic states are alert, relaxed, concentrated, and unconscious.

These states of consciousness take many forms and we move through them naturally within every twenty-four hour cycle. You probably have states you prefer more than others. Depending on the state you naturally migrate to, will determine the type of person you are. You may be a dreamer and highly imaginative, analytical, or a physical person with good alert focus, each requiring a different state of consciousness. No matter what your primary state of mind is, you can learn to be flexible and alter your state of consciousness at any time. This is important because various states of mind are needed for various tasks.

Writing a term paper requires a different state of mind than meditation. Relaxing with friends requires a different state of mind than running a marathon race. Most of us have certain states that are easy to create and other states that are difficult. An executive, who has been poring over reports all day, may find it hard to relax when arriving home. An athletic type with super alert physical focus, may not enjoy the imaginative state of mind required to write a novel.

When a state of mind is difficult for us to create, it is because it is not our natural signature pattern. The way we have learned to use our consciousness will contribute as well. It is often necessary to strengthen those areas that are weak. If you are a day dreamy person, you may need to train your mind to be more focused. On the other hand, if you are highly stimulated by your surroundings, you may need to learn how to relax. If you stay in deep concentrated states of mind, it would be good for you to get out of your thoughts and observe the world around you.

Most of my classes focus on helping people find ways to let go of the physical boundaries of thought, and access that intuitive side of consciousness. In doing this, I have had to learn about the various states which can be measured through brain wave study. The brain will exhibit various frequencies at an alert, restful, deep concentration, and unconscious state. The more flexible we are the easier it is to move from one of these states to the next with ease. When our brain wave pattern exhibits the same frequency as someone else's, they are said to be in synchronicity with one another. This creates a resonance between them.

As was talked about earlier, studies show when a mother is quietly nursing her baby, she will often synchronize her brain wave patterns with the baby. A newborn baby exhibits an enormous amount of slow, nearly unconscious brain waves, causing them to sleep most of the time. The mother's normal brain wave patterns are far different than her new born baby's as she goes about her day. Even though she may show some patterns like her baby throughout the day, normally she would not experience the slow delta wave in her waking state. However, while nursing, she is able to alter her normal pattern and flexibly move her consciousness to match her new born baby's. This creates an intuitive connection between mother and child.

In other studies, they have found people most flexible in consciousness, have the best overall opportunity for success. The reason is they are more balanced in the use of their mind and can adapt to the state that is needed at the time. Imagine being hyper alert to your physical surroundings when you need to narrow your focus and concentrate. This is what occurs for those suffering from attention deficit disorder or ADD. Work has begun in this area to help children shift their state of consciousness to be more settled. This is done through brain wave feedback rather than drugs. A friend of mine works in this field and is thrilled with the promising results.

The ability to create a needed state of consciousness at will is helpful to anyone. This requires knowledge of the various states and the flexibility to shift your consciousness. My work primarily involves teaching one to shift to an intuitive state of consciousness. I want to discuss the slower unconscious brain waves because that is what is found to be the source of intuition. Access to this state usually takes training, because when one is in this state, they are unconscious. However, one can train themselves to have awareness at this state of mind. It requires a relaxed consciousness, working in harmony with the slower near unconscious state.

EEG RESULTS

After my training in hypnosis, I recognized my ability to shift through the various states of consciousness at will. I could feel these shifts in my body and mind, however, I had no proof of this other than the sensations I felt. I believed I was shifting into a slow brain wave state, nearing unconsciousness, when I did the health intuitive sessions. It became important for me to know if this was true. Only an EEG could show if this was so.

As usual, once I began to think about what I needed, the opportunity was presented. I was giving a lecture at a bookstore in a neighboring state one Saturday. I was a bit disappointed when only three people attended, but continued with the lecture as usual. I ended by giving each person a short health intuitive session at the end.

Alice, the only woman in class, came up to me afterwards explaining how she was part of an organization doing studies on subtle healing energy. She was in charge of the research on brainwave activity and asked if I would consider being one of her research subjects. It would involve a day at their research lab having an EEG to show what happened to my brain waves during an intuitive session. Of course I was more than happy to volunteer, since this was exactly what I had been asking of the universe.

The facility was located some three hours from my home. I arose early, showered, and started the long drive arriving before ten a.m. The Ozark Research Institute housed a three story brick building in downtown Fayetteville, Arkansas. The main floor of the building was home to the offices, bookstore, meditation, and healing rooms. Upstairs was a media room where videos could be viewed of all the teachers and healers that had passed through this institution. In the basement was an extensive library, sensory deprivation tank, a large circular color therapy wheel, a sound therapy machine, and several other pieces of equipment I didn't recognize. At the far end of the hall was a large room where I would spend most of the day. It was a spacious room with a recliner, EEG equipment, and computer at one end.

We started immediately after lunch. In order for the EEG sensors to have good receptivity, it required a clean head of hair free of any oils or chemicals. Since I had used a conditioner on my hair that morning, a shower was in order. I was a little uncomfortable stripping off in the large open therapy room with the sensory deprivation tank and color wheel, but that was where the shower was located, obviously an after thought added for the purpose of doing EEGs.

With clean hair, I sat in the recliner while Alice and Ray spread a clear gel over my head. A cap with small strategically placed holes was then pulled tightly over my scalp. Tiny electronic sensors were inserted in the cap making certain to have good electrical contact with my brain waves. Once we began the EEG, a read out would show up on the computer monitor and be stored in the system.

They wanted a test of my natural brain wave signature and asked me to do several things before the health intuitive session. I looked at a white wall, read a few pages from a book, relaxed, and finally they asked that I project healing to someone.

Once they had all of these brain wave readings documented, it was time to start the health intuitive session. We decided to use Ray's wife as my subject. I started my descent, shifting my brain waves down to a very slow near unconscious state, to connect intuitively with her. I repeated her name to myself as I moved my attention to focus only on her.

I could tell as I passed through the various brain wave levels starting from the fully alert state of beta, shifting to the relaxed alpha state, moving into the subconscious concentrated state of theta, and finally arriving at the near unconscious state of delta. The familiar changes I could feel in my body and mind were present, only this time it was being monitored, recorded, and witnessed.

Once I felt connected with Ray's wife, I knew I was in the delta state. My brain waves showed this very slow frequency on the EEG and my body felt the high electrical current and slow mental processing. From this state, I perceive the intuitive signals. I feel no separation between the information I am seeking and my own thoughts at this level.

Subtle impressions began to flow into my awareness regarding Ray's wife. I moved to the faster theta state to form a structured sentence from the impressions. From there, I directed my mind to move into the alpha state in order to feel her emotions. If I had been allowed to speak during the EEG, I would have shared the information with Ray and Alice.

I continued to move back and forth, from the slow delta state to the faster theta and alpha states, as I received new information and then formed a structure of these impressions in my mind. I could feel the shift in electrical current and the speed of my mental processing as I continued to do the health intuitive session for Ray's wife. I had always been perceptive of this process, but now it was being observed and recorded.

Alice shared the EEG read out with me as soon as I returned from washing the goop out of my hair which required my third shower of the day. It was exactly as I suspected. My brain waves performed in direct correlation to the sensations I felt in my body and mind. The intuitive signal or impression came to me while in a slow delta state, and meaningful structure was created in my mind at the faster theta and alpha states.

I had the proof I was seeking and was now endowed with new teaching material. I could help my students reach that intuitive state by teaching them how to be flexible and achieve these varying states of consciousness.

I had also observed a real shift in my heart over the years during the intuitive process. I described it as reaching a deep state of compassion. There was always a connection of love for my clients, and a sensation of humbleness in my heart, just before an impression was received. I looked to recreate this state each time, knowing it would get me to the place I needed to be in order to connect with the information. Later, Alice shared with me how her research had discovered the heart waves have a tremendous influence over the brain.

INTUITION REQUIRES FLEXIBILITY

Teaching people to be intuitive requires them to be flexible and shift their state of consciousness to receive an intuitive signal. Once they receive this signal from the very slow brain waves, they move to a more rapid brain wave pattern in order to interpret the signal. This is easy for some but others must work hard to accomplish this.

Fear of stepping out of known states, finding no motivation for change, and seeing little value in developing a flexible consciousness, are the reasons most stay in the narrow band they are currently using. The superstitions associated with some states of consciousness also contribute to the taboo of entering such states. Yet when analyzed, even with logical intelligence, it appears there are great benefits to developing a flexible mind.

In the work place, it has been long assumed if you have the technical skill to perform a task, you will make a great employee. Today, there is the recognition of emotional and people skills being equally important. I once worked for a company with a fellow employee who liked to keep things stirred up. He was always finding some kind of fault with the business and the management. He did little to lift anyone's spirits. His attitude, however, did not hamper his job performance. He was punctual, performed well, and seldom missed a day of work. By all evaluation standards, he was a good employee. But he was not a team player, and that bled over to influence everyone. He was miserable, and he tried to make everyone else feel the same.

He failed to have a bond, brain wave synchronicity, with the ideals of the company. His inability to be flexible and empathize with the firm was obvious. He selfishly complained to co-workers which cost the company many a good employee. Mind flexibility, at the heart of the employees, can make or break a firm's success.

How many times have you seen a relationship dissolve because a couple grows apart. If their brain waves were tested, it would no doubt show some serious difference in the two as this change occurs. The ability to mentally synchronize with those we love is vital to holding a relationship together. If there is change and growth by one and not the other, it is uncomfortable because what was once in sync is no longer. With a flexible mind, one is capable of synchronizing with anyone at will. That doesn't mean a relationship that has grown out of sync will stay together, but it does mean you have more ability to adapt to the change. When a relationship, be it personal or professional, is in sync, it creates the resonance needed to be compatible.

How often have you watched a good friend repeat a destructive pattern in their life again and again? They are always with the wrong person, fighting with their spouse, or spend to the point they can not make their cash flow meet their bills. This person is fixed in a problem, so it plays like an old, stuck record. They remain rigid in their patterns so nothing changes until they can finally break free and learn there is another way. This is a prime candidate to develop mind flexibility. By learning to shift their awareness from one state to another, it allows them to see things differently. They are no longer stuck in just one way of thinking, nor in one way of behaving.

Flexible states of consciousness are easy to reach, but few are aware of them. Most consider personality traits something they were born with, and many are born with very fixed mind patterns. For those who are, it may be a difficult path. They may be very narrow in their views and do not adapt well to change.

Developing a flexible consciousness is taking control of your state of mind at will. Imagine relaxing at the moment you need it most. Imagine being tired and yet able to create alertness. Imagine being relaxed and moving easily and quickly into a state of full concentration. And finally, imagine being fully awake and conscious, and shift directly into the unconscious intuitive levels, and retrieve a piece of information from the resources available there.

I have learned the value of a flexible mind. I had a friend once that liked to play chess. I played but never had the ability to win against this person. One day I decided to experiment with a concentrated and strategic mental state while playing chess. I challenged my friend to a regular Sunday evening game for several weeks. Before each game I would move to the concentrated state of theta. I directed my mind to be aware of the big picture of the game and make moves from this level of mind. I won every game we played, a first for me.

Chapter Fourteen

LET ME SHARE

TEACHING

I am a teacher at heart, always wanting to share information, and give others the benefit of what I have learned. Through my years of gaining self-awareness, developing my intuition, and discovering the greatness of human potential, I did a great deal of reading. I ran across two books that helped me immensely. One shared information about the mind/body relationship, and the other explained how spiritual maturity is part of a physical process.

I wanted very much to share this information, however it did not fit with the only course I was teaching at that time, hypnosis. I kept the idea in the back of my mind, always looking for a way. When I created my health intuitive course, which is one of many I offer today, I used the books as guides and they are included as text books for the course.

Over the years, many courses have been added to the certification course in hypnosis. I also offer home study courses in remote viewing, health intuitive, and a manifestation course, along with a variety of workshops and classes in person.

The birth of each course came from an intuitive moment of inspiration. The timing was right, the knowledge was there, and the students were asking for what I had to offer. As I share how the courses came about, keep in mind my life has been guided. Maybe not so much from some great spirit, but from some intuitive place inside me that knows.

THE HEALTH INTUITIVE COURSE IS BORN

"It sounds like the voice of God," Joyce said. Theresa's sister, Joyce, was in the states visiting from South America, where her husband worked for the U.S. government. I had known Theresa, a devoted client, for a long time but never met her sister Joyce, until now. Over the years, I had met most of Theresa's siblings, as well as her parents. She came from a large family who were all very intuitive at birth. Many of them were in the medical profession and were very interested in my health intuitive work. Theresa wanted Joyce to have a health intuitive session before leaving the country and returning home.

We sat in my family room getting to know one another. As I did the health intuitive session for Joyce, the information flowed well, a sign we were in resonance. When I finished, she thanked me and they left. A short time later Theresa called very excited. Her sister was very impressed. She then told me how her sister thought the session sounded like the voice of God. I was a little shocked and very humbled by the idea.

Sometimes people idealize the intuitive process and place the one delivering the message on some kind of enlightened pedestal. Joyce's comment made me realize I needed to share with others how this is done. Because I learned to be an intuitive, rather than being born one, I understood it was my discipline and practice that enabled me to do it. I had worked very hard learning to be a health intuitive. I knew it was a skill and I certainly wasn't any more enlightened than anyone else. At that moment, I felt I must teach this process to others.

I knew it would be a challenge to construct a health intuitive training course. My own process had taken years of self-analysis before I even attempted to do a session for someone else. I had studied my thoughts and emotions for a long time, observing how they had a short and long term effect on my body. This time spent understanding the relationship between the spiritual, mental, emotional, and physical parts of myself, had been a vital part of my learning. I needed to give my students the benefit of this understanding.

YOUR BODY TELLS A STORY

For several years I used the health intuitive process for myself. It was a self-realization program I developed for my own enlightenment. I let my body be my guide, spending time each day listening to its needs. I became very sensitive to my physical system, noticing changes like stress, tension, pain and congestion at the slightest onset. When I listened, I was able to understand how my body was constantly responding to my thoughts, feelings, and every situation of my life.

With the aid of the two books I mentioned earlier and my own intuition, I began to see the direct correlation between the varied parts of myself. I then worked on changing my physical condition through changing my thoughts and feelings. As my emotions and thoughts changed, my body changed. I could feel the stress, tension, and pain leave as these patterns were altered.

I began noticing tension if I became frustrated, sluggishness when I became sad, and nervousness when I became indecisive. My spirit was letting me know I needed to alter my thought patterns and emotions. My body became the messenger of my spirit causing me to feel more spiritually connected. My health improved, but more than that, my mental and emotional well being improved. There was a consensus built between the spiritual, mental, emotional and physical parts of myself.

I never felt as though I were being chastised by my spirit just because I had an ache or a pain. Spirit wasn't judging my imperfections. On the contrary, I knew and accepted my humanness. As long as I was in the body, I would have physical conditions because I am not perfect. I felt blessed that my body was a reminder to me that there was a better way to respond. When I chose to think in loving, caring ways, my body responded in the same manner. I had less stress, less pain, and less illness. It was that simple.

The more I used my body as a spiritual messenger, the more information flowed. It became second nature to me, and later this became my health intuitive process. It was a guiding resource for my own evolvement. It wasn't just about my health, even though my health greatly improved, it was a daily spiritual practice, enabling me to understand how spirit was reflected in every cell of my body.

Integration, rather than separation, was the result of my efforts. Separation is a trademark of allopathic medicine. The body is divided like a gigantic puzzle with a specialist for each part. Then there are specialist among specialist for the more intricate workings of the various systems. We view the psyche as separate from the physical body, and the spirit yet separate from that.

There are religious leaders for spiritual guidance, psychologists for emotional guidance, and physicians for physical guidance. Each have their own expertise. We are whole beings, however, and these parts interact. We must learn to integrate these separate parts into a single working whole, without an expert advisor to help us figure out this integrative process.

The time I spent studying my personal mind/body

relationship helped me to see how these parts are connected. They communicate and are interdependent. I began to understand the areas of my life that needed improvement through the way my body responded. I made changes based on this awareness. My life and health improved. I will spend a lifetime making changes as new situations are presented, and I continue to understand myself more.

The health intuitive process is not about physical health, but it is about wholeness. A health intuitive session is far more spiritual than physical. It can guide you to self-understanding and give you advice on how to make your life whole again.

THE COURSE IS CONSTRUCTED

I had no idea where to begin when I put the health intuitive course together. The outline included twelve body systems, foods, quantum mechanics of healing, the mind/body relationship, a review of twelve health intuitive sessions, and the development of intuition. I included a structured format helping my students to organize the information.

I decided in order to understand intuition, the students needed to understand more about the autonomic system of the body. The chakra system, referred to in Eastern philosophy, gives a good explanation of the correlating areas of the body and thought. The crisscrossing pattern of nerves along the spinal column that form seven intersections relate to the seven chakras in the body. The chakra centers correlate to various areas of the body, and each carries a certain emotional make up and thought pattern.

My first class, consisted of six students, whom I knew from intuitive sessions or previous classes. Being my first health intuitive class, we all learned together.

We met once a week for eighteen weeks. The first five weeks consisted of lectures and exercises. On the sixth class, they were given their first challenging assignment of doing a real health intuitive session. I gave them the name of a person they did not know. They were to do a health intuitive session for this subject, transcribe it, and bring it to class the next week.

Without diagnosing, they were to describe any problems seen in the subject's physical body. They were to trace the emotions and thought patterns contributing to this physical disorder and describe that, as well.

The students' transcripts were brought to class and read out loud for everyone to hear. We compared each of them, one to another, looking for any correlating information to help us verify if it was correct. I also did a session for comparison.

The students were doing the sessions at different times and not comparing notes until class time. From the very first transcript read, it was evident they were all looking at the same person. One student might see excess fluid around the knee and the next transcript would talk about the same condition. The same was true of thoughts and emotions. This followed week after week.

It was extremely good for the students to hear one another's transcripts. It helped them accept the accuracy of their own sessions. I also had a health review from the subject helping us confirm what the students were seeing. This gave more validation to the information.

The comparison process worked. They were able to quickly tell if they were receiving intuitive information or not. The course was very hands on, not just lecture based, so the students were prepared to do intuitive sessions upon graduation.

REBELLIOUS INTUITIVE

There is always one rebellious student in every class. In the first health intuitive class, that student was Leonard. He was a middle aged man, who worked in an office by day, and enjoyed metaphysical classes by night. He had studied applied metaphysics and reiki, but didn't think of himself as being intuitive. He wanted to learn how to be a health intuitive which brought him to my class.

When I gave the students their first intuitive session, Leonard wrote down the name enthusiastically. The next week he returned to class and listened as the others read their transcripts. When it was his turn, he politely said he tried, but did not get anything in the session. He had nothing to share with us.

I encouraged him to try again the next week with the new name. As long as he followed the procedure he had learned in class, he should get some intuitive information. He once again enthusiastically took the name home.

The following week I heard the same story from Leonard. He had tried to do the session but did not receive any information. I was uncertain how to advise him and suggested he try several times throughout the week. If he didn't receive information the first time, I was hoping he would on the second or third try. Maybe the persistence would work.

The following week the class gathered at the usual seven o'clock time. The students had completed their third health intuitive session for the course. We usually began the class by having each student read their transcripts outloud. This week I decided to delay the readings. I was curious to know if Leonard had done the session this week. He had not. For the third week in a row, he had nothing to share. His attempt had failed again.

I was a bit puzzled about what to do. I wanted Leonard to learn how to receive intuitive information. After all, that was his purpose in taking the course. He wanted to be a health intuitive. I felt responsible to help him, but for the life of me, did not know how to get him there.

It was obvious, just telling him to do the session wasn't working, so I requested he come to the front of the class. I asked him to sit beside my desk and handed him a pen and paper. I then had him say the subjects name out loud. Meanwhile I intuitively connected with Leonard's mind and the subject. I was hoping to create a sort of three way intuitive conference call between us.

Having done intuitive sessions for years, I knew exactly what to do once connected. The trick was getting Leonard to intuitively follow my lead.

I asked him to write down three areas of the body. It could be anything like the heart, eyes, or joints. He wasn't to think about it, just do it. I then asked him to write down a few symptoms one might experience in these areas. He objected, but I told him to just make it up if nothing came to mind. We ended with the emotions and thoughts contributing to these problems. He was obedient to my requests, but frankly, both of us thought this might be a waste of time.

I picked up the paper and handed it to him telling him this would serve as his health intuitive transcript for this week. It was short and incomplete but it would do. Even if the information was wrong, it would get him over this hurdle of having nothing to present.

The students read their sessions out loud. I listened for anything that Leonard had written down. One by one we heard all the items listed on his paper. The intuitive conference call had worked. Leonard was able to get intuitive information.

I was quite surprised as was he. No doubt it had helped to verbally direct him through the process, but more important than that, I had intuitively connected with his mind. I now know an intuitive connection is just as powerful as a verbal one.

I learned a very important part of teaching that day. As an instructor, it is just as important to teach from the silence of my intuition, as it is to organize good verbal lectures.

Leonard also learned how easy it was to be intuitive. His fears and doubts about doing a session were removed. The next week he came with transcript in hand, proud to read it to the rest of the class. Only this week, I had a surprise for the group.

Previous to this class, the students never met the subjects. They did each health intuitive session without the subject being present. This week I invited the subject, a woman in her forties, to class to evaluate the transcripts herself. What better way to give them feedback than from the one they were intuitively reading.

Her name was Marilyn. I introduced her to the class and gathered the students' transcripts. I led her to my office where she was to go over every drop of information. I left her alone to mull over the papers. While she assessed the students work, I went back to class and gave the lecture for the week.

A couple of hours passed before I retrieved Marilyn from my office. She was just completing the final transcript as I opened the door. We returned to the classroom where the students anxiously awaited her comments.

She hesitated, then began with Leonard's transcript. Her comments surprised all of us. After reading each of the six transcripts carefully, Leonard's was the most accurate.

The rebellious student had now moved to the top of the class. He had been so intimidated about doing a session, but once he overcame his fears, he was very good. The entire class was happy for him. They had witnessed his challenge and his accomplishment.

Many students have the same issue as Leonard. Often when a student first starts speaking, they are intimidated and do not want to be embarrassed. It is something everyone must get over. If the information is correct, it is wonderful. If the information is wrong, then we work on getting them to the right information. It is all part of the learning process.

I often share Leonard's story with new students. Some students have a hard time trusting intuitive thoughts. They just assume they are making it up. I want to caution about being assumptive because it can happen. But I also encourage students to have the courage to speak. Once they are willing to open up and do the session, they find the rest is easy.

Yes, it often feels like there is nothing to say. There is no intuitive message until you give it your voice and then it flows. The more you use it the more it improves. The first step is to trust and speak.

What prevents the student from speaking is the ego. Most of us are afraid to be wrong. It is embarrassing. When using your intuitive voice, it is like skydiving without a parachute. You jump off into an open clouded sky with no bearings. You say all of these things, that you have no way of verifying, while you are saying them. Everything feels like you are making it up, adding to the foolishness you are sensing.

You must be willing to be wrong, but you also must accept that you may be right. Either way it requires trust. Once you have developed your intuitive voice and know your accuracy rate, it is easier. You learn to trust the process without relying on your five senses and your analytical mind. After a time, the unfamiliar resource of intuition becomes familiar and not so strange. It no longer feels like you are jumping off into unknown territory, but is a familiar sea of great wisdom, knowledge, and insight.

SYNCHRONICITY SPARKS A NEW COURSE

I was in meditation asking about the make up of the universe when I was told there were many universes. Life within each universe feeds energy to the next universe. Each of us produce some type of energy. The analogy of fruit trees came to mind. The same way there are many varieties of fruit trees there are many varieties of energies produced by life forms. I then asked what type of fruit tree I might be. The answer came back very quickly, pear.

My meditation ended but I continued to think about the possibilities of this information. The thought of producing energy that feeds another universe was a really farfetched idea and one that was hard for me to accept. I didn't give it much significance, suspecting it was just a symbolic idea that came to my mind.

Later that day, I visited a local book store. Knowing the employees as well as I do there, it wasn't surprising one handed me a book she thought I might like. It was a new arrival, not even on the shelves yet.

To be polite, I took the book and opened it to a random page. There in bold capital letters was the word PEAR. I glanced to the next page and again there was PEAR. Every page I turned to was the word PEAR. I turned the book over and saw the title was *Remote Perception*. It was a book about remote viewing. Odd that she handed me this book considering I had been thinking about creating a new class in remote viewing. It seemed quite synchronistic since pear was the earlier focus of my meditation.

I suspected this had all come together to encourage me to get back to work. Up to this point, I had only contemplated teaching this new course, because I was returning back to work after a prolonged absence. I was just coming out of my healing crises and needed to teach again.

The first step was finding a place to hold the class. I wanted a good size room that was also very private in order to avoid any distractions. There needed to be enough space to use my projector, have ample tables for students, and a pleasant atmosphere. On top of this, it needed to be affordable.

I started looking through the yellow pages for conference centers and meeting rooms. I discovered an ad for the Ambassador Inn, listing a conference room as one of their amenities. I called and found they could set it up in the manner I needed, plus they were willing to give me an affordable rate. Of course I wanted to see the room before reserving it for the class. I grabbed the information I had taken over the phone and headed for the hotel. As I approached the area, I started looking for the Ambassador Inn but couldn't find it. I drove back and forth where I felt it should be but no sign of the Ambassador Inn. I finally gave up and drove back home.

Once I arrived home, I immediately thumbed through the phonebook to find the ad again. I found the ad and read the address. It was right in the area I had been looking. How could I have missed it? I called them again and they politely told me the name of the hotel had changed but assured me it was at the same address.

I drove back across town. Finding the address right away this time, I went inside where I was shown the conference room. It was more than satisfactory with plenty of room and quiet. I reserved it on the spot.

As I drove out of the parking lot, the name of the hotel suddenly hit me. I had just reserved a room at the PEAR TREE INN. What are the odds of that? All in a single day, my meditation drew me to focus on pear, I was handed a book on remote viewing with the bold letters PEAR, and now the name of the hotel where my first remote viewing class would be held was Pear Tree Inn. Humorously, I wondered if there was a pear shortage in the universe.

PREPARING FOR CLASS

This being my first class since my healing crises, I was concerned about my stamina. I would be standing eight hours a day for five days. I honestly didn't know if I could do it. My body was weak and I knew this would be challenging to my nervous system. I felt as though I had to give it a try even if it was difficult to endure.

I started preparing the course material, intuitively looking at the best way to teach this unique method of accessing intuition. I was shown how everything in the universe breaks down into smaller and smaller parts, and this was a good approach for remote viewing. I designed the course, placed ads around the state, and waited to see what happened.

One day I got a call from a young man inquiring about the course. He wanted to register and was filled with questions. After a time, he informed me he was with the United States Intelligence Department. I was concerned the timing of the course might not fit with his rigid military schedule, but he assured me they would cooperate with giving him time off for the course. I suspected the course was an assignment, rather than of personal interest, but I couldn't prove that. I had to wonder if the class was being investigated by the government?

The first day of class he walked in and I immediately knew him. He was physically fit, with short hair and straight shoulders. He was younger than most of the other students. Throughout the class, he did not cease asking questions. He wanted to know everything about my training, where I had studied, how I learned to be so good, how he could get in touch with other remote viewers. I was polite and answered his questions honestly.

I observed him in class and noticed his skill as a remote viewer was excellent, even though he pretended to know very little. He was just too good for this to be his first class. I suspected he was trying to look like a beginner but was well trained as a remote viewer.

The class ended after five days and the students had to say goodby to one another. Before leaving, he wanted to get a picture of the whole group. I have taught a lot of classes in my life, but this was the first time anyone had asked to take a group picture at the end. I guess those military guys are just sentimental.

MANIFESTATION AWARENESS

As I said earlier, all my courses have been inspired. The few that have not just do not seem to work out. I have learned to listen and only create courses I am intuitively led to develop.

The inspiration for the manifestation course came about in a convertible sports car. I was talking about metaphysics when my friend asked if I would teach a class on the subject. I was reluctant, but decided to do it as an experiment. Later, it became my course on spiritual manifestation, and one I am very proud of.

I personally learned the most from this course. Maybe because I created it from week to week and pushed the limits of what I knew how to do. It was an experimental, free class that lasted nearly two years. This gave me the time and liberty to play with intuition, synchronicity, and manifestation.

I wanted to capture the same amazing ability with manifestation as I had with intuitive communication. At some point, I realized it is just as easy to communicate a request which reshapes your life as it is to receive intuitive information. I started the manifestation course, with little understanding of this, and finished with a whole set of procedures to create positive synchronicity, and manifest your desires.

THE WAVE

Most classes have a range of students that go from doing well to being mediocre. The health intuitive students seem to fare a bit better than the remote viewing students. I believe this is because they are aiming at using what they are learning, where many of the remote viewing students are just curious.

Occasionally, I will have a student that achieves optimum intuitive performance in class. I call this optimum experience riding the intuitive wave. Most students have nice intuitive experiences, which is different than experiencing this wave.

Riding the intuitive wave is like surfing in the ocean. You find the wave you are looking for and then you let the wave carry you to shore. When you are on the wave, you know it. You are very connected to the information flowing through you. It flows so fast and so confidently there can be no doubt. The words come to you and it is as though you are speaking from some place that is not earthbound. You are in complete resonance with the information.

One student was able to ride this wave successfully during her very first class. I knew it immediately by the tone of her voice and the rhythm of her words. Every word she spoke was profound and to the point. It took the rest of the class a little while to recognize the level she had reached. Once they became aware, they understood what I had been telling them about riding the intuitive wave.

When she opened her eyes, she looked amazed as did the rest of us. She knew she had truly connected with a resource beyond her own knowledge. Her body, mind, and spirit were in complete harmony with the subject. It was as though there was no separation between her whole being and the information that was flowing from her mouth. Her personal identity stepped out of the way as she became the wave she was riding.

The intuitive wave is what a student is looking for as they practice the intuitive process. Knowing the accuracy of the information you are delivering is extremely satisfying. When I am connected to this level of intuition, I feel completely peaceful. Every part of my body feels exalted in a state of complete bliss.

Once I discovered this wave, it was easy to recreate. Words flow very easily from this state, and match well with the intent of the intuitive session, making the information more accurate. Heart and brain waves feel like they are in synchronicity with one another, creating a deep compassion and love between my client and myself. This wave seems to harmonize with some spiritual part of ourselves. To ride this wave, is like reaching a pure state of consciousness, that only holds the best of intent for both the intuitive and the client. That is why it is so healing for me to do an intuitive session. I come out renewed in my spirit. No matter what kind of day I am having, I always come out of an intuitive session feeling better. Love just seems to permeate my being after riding this intuitive wave.

I share the intuitive wave model with my students to establish a goal for them as they learn. They work to develop their intuition knowing the wave is out there to be discovered. Once this happens, they have arrived at intuitive knowing. They have achieved the most harmonious and connected state of integration with the process that can be achieved. It is a total fusing process with the subject and the information you are seeking.

Chapter Fifteen

90 DAYS TO INTUITION

HOW TO BE INTUITIVE

Basic intuitive perception can be learned with practice. The information comes into your awareness the same way information travels through your five senses, only there is not supporting evidence. The continuous sensory signal, as when you are looking at an image or listening to a song, is not present. You must learn to attentively recognize the signal and remember the impression.

The beginning of all intuition is to have an open mind and know you really can perceive intuitively. This is true even when the information is ambiguous. This can be discouraging to some who want it to be as clear as the five senses. Think of it like a small sound you hear in the night. You awake not sure of the sound's origin. It is a vague echo at that point, and difficult to place in context to your environment.

Many intuitive impressions are very short and subtle, leaving you in doubt of the signal. This is why one must learn how to decipher what is really part of the impression, and what your mind wants to contribute, in order to make it meaningful. This makes the information less contaminated by your personal thoughts. Often times, one receives intuitive information, but it is not identified because they add far too much imagination with it. This negates the impression and causes all of it to be doubted.

LEARNING THE FIVE SKILLS OF INTUITION

Intuition requires five mental skills. They are sensitivity, communication, focus, undivided attention, and receptivity. Other areas that are helpful are objectivity, good memory, detail orientation, and the ability to separate mental information from an emotional sensation.

SENSITIVITY

Sensitivity is developed through learning to be receptive to the five senses, then clearly defining each sensation in detail. The skill of accurate and clear sensory perception creates accurate and clear reception of the subtle intuitive impression. The intuitive impressions often travel through the five senses or what seems like sensory stimulation. It is at an autonomic level, but may be strong enough to create some sort of sensation in the body. A brief visual image may occur. This is often so brief, however, it is almost not recognizable. An odor, touch, sound or taste may all happen while receiving an intuitive impression.

The remote viewing course I teach takes you through all five senses asking for information about what is called a target. The target is the object, place, event, or person being viewed that is beyond the range of the five senses. Even though the target is not within the scope of the five senses, the target will have information attached to it just the same as if you were physically present. When you are able to accurately describe a target, you know you are intuitively receiving information.

As I teach my students sensitivity, I have discovered some basic obstacles. First, many people do not have strong sense detection. In other words, they have trouble identifying certain tastes or smells. They may have a dull sense of vision or not recall visual things well. The same may be true of sounds and textures. Those who are not acutely aware of their senses must develop this prior to being intuitive.

I enhanced my sensory awareness, prior to becoming intuitive, by practicing each day. I once did this while eating a peach. The contrast of the soft fuzzy peel against the hard knife handle, the fresh peach aroma filling the air, and the slight dripping sounds of the juices, as I peeled the fruit over the sink, would have gone unnoticed if not for this exercise. Thoughts of other things would have filled my mind.

There is a very simple exercise to help you improve sensitivity. Take five minutes a day and describe your surroundings using only your five senses. Separate your emotional reactions from the data you receive. Do not describe how you feel about the sky being blue, only that it is blue. Limit your awareness to only sensory information. Doing this exercise often will increase your sensory awareness and will improve your intuitive sessions.

COMMUNICATION

Clear and accurate exchange of information is one definition of communication. Once you have received an intuitive impression, it is then important to clearly and accurately describe it. If you do not have this ability, the impression will be lost in an unclear attempt to communicate. This is both true of your inner communication to yourself, and your communication to others.

I take my students through a communication evaluation. This helps them understand their personal communication style. They may discover they are overly descriptive and thoroughly communicate their ideas, or they may find they leave out information and short change communication when they speak. Some have found they do not listen well. Some are very assumptive and only halfway listen to what others say, while a few are very exact with communication.

Ask yourself these simple questions to know your communication style. Do you dominate a conversation? Do you interrupt others while they are speaking? Are you quiet and polite while listening? Do you ask for clarification when uncertain what someone is trying to say? Do your thoughts drift causing you to think about other things while listening? Are you able to accurately repeat what someone has told you? Do you think about your choice of words before speaking? Do your words accurately describe what you are trying to say? Are you thinking about your response to another person while they are speaking? How often do you have misunderstandings?

I have learned to stop and match my words with what I truly mean to say. I wait for a clear thought before speaking. Speaking in unclear or partial sentences prohibits good communication. Making assumptions, while listening to others, is also dangerous.

Communication comes down to the simple ability to clearly listen and clearly express. Once you recognize your weaknesses in this area, you can begin to improve. The start of this is recognition. Know what makes for good communication, and start practicing that in day to day life.

The degree of communication skill you already have will be reflected in your intuitive sessions. An ability to listen to someone speak will equate to the ability to listen to an intuitive impression. Likewise, if you have difficulty in accurately describing your thoughts, you will most likely have difficulty in describing an intuitive impression.

FOCUS

Focus is a concentrated mental effort directing attention. When a camera lens is in focus, it means there is a clear view of whatever it is aimed toward. When your mind is focused, it is clearly concentrating on something.

You focus on a book, when you read, so as to clearly see the words on a page and correctly interpret them. You focus your mind when driving to avoid an accident. And you focus when you are learning a new skill in order to remember the information. This focus is necessary for good mental perception. The more you are able to focus, the more optimum is your concentration.

Focus is easy when you are interested in the subject. It takes little effort to focus on things you enjoy. The entertainment value of a subject rewards you with pleasure when concentrating. My twelve year old nephew can focus for hours on an electronic game, but when given homework that is less appealing, it may take far more effort to focus.

In order to focus intuitively, one must be very dedicated. After all, you are focusing on the complete unknown. There is little pleasure to hold your attention unless you can retrieve accurate information. This is why you must be able to focus your mind even when it isn't enjoyable. The more disciplined you are with mental focus, the easier it will be to consistently concentrate during an intuitive session.

Combine the sensitivity exercise with a focus exercise. While describing an object like a pencil, note how focused you are on the object. Describe it in detail using all five senses, but be aware of how you are focused on the object while doing this. When you have completed the sensory exercise, close your eyes and once again pore over all the details of the pencil. Keep yourself concentrating on every detail, even long after you have lost interest in the information. This will give you greater focus ability, and teach you the discipline of concentration.

RECEPTIVITY

To be receptive is to be open to an impression. Your mind has the ability to be either aggressively active or passively receptive. We live in a world that promotes aggressive use of the mind, but little is taught on the skill of receptivity. If I ask you to think about a subject, you most likely would not have difficulty doing so. However, if I requested that your mind go blank and become receptive, you might have more of a challenge reaching this state.

Think of your mind as something that can be active or at rest. Like a muscle that is in movement, it must contract and use energy in order to cause the motion. When at rest, there is no movement. When you are thinking, you are aggressively activating your thoughts. When you listen openly, your mind is passive and receptive to information.

An exercise which demonstrates this state of mind is to take a pen and paper and write the following sentence.

Mary has a puppy.

After you have completed writing this sentence, think up a sentence of your own and write it down. Do this several times and note the difference between the two activities. Your mind is in an aggressive, thinking state when asked to think of a sentence. You must change to a receptive state of mind when receiving a sentence already prepared for you.

The belief that it is better to give than to receive is part of our mental conditioning. It is actually difficult to give if you haven't first received. When mentally receptive, great ideas come to mind. Most inventors have learned to appreciate the receptive qualities of their mind, because it gives them their creativity.

Learning how to create a passive, receptive state of mind is vital to the skill of intuition. One must be receptive to the subtle intuitive impressions in order to perceive them. If your mind is aggressively thinking, the intuitive impressions will be lost. Letting your mind be passive, receptive, and still is one of the most challenging obstacles to developing the intuitive skill.

Practice listening without injecting your personal thoughts or opinions. Practice stilling your mind through meditation. Listen to music. Try only hearing the sounds without emotionally responding or letting memory flood your thoughts. A receptive mind has no judgment or opinion, it only records what is given.

UNDIVIDED ATTENTION

Attention can be picked up and moved like a paperweight sitting on a desk. It is under your direction and will. Notice how you have chosen to place your attention on the pages of this book. Now take your attention off the book for a moment and look up, giving your attention to something around you. When you are ready, bring your attention back to the pages of this book. This is how easy it is to move your attention.

Undivided attention is a bit more complicated. It requires holding attention, without moving it, for some time. Even if the phone rings, or the dog barks, when you have undivided attention, your thoughts will remain at a single point. To practice undivided attention, narrow your awareness to something and hold your attention there. Notice if your mind wants to wander to other things. If it does, you have broken undivided attention.

Many of my students have difficulty knowing how to direct their mental attention. They think of a thousand things during a twenty minute meditation. They have trouble even staying with one of the five senses when describing an impression.

An exercise good for developing undivided attention is to light a candle and place it on a table in front of you about two feet away. Place a blank piece of paper between you and the candle. While placing your undivided attention on the candle, time yourself for ten minutes. During that ten minute time frame, think of nothing other than the candle flame. If any thought or sensation, unrelated to the candle, comes into your awareness, make a check mark on the paper in front of you.

If you think of something other than the candle, you have broken your attention. At that point, gently bring your thoughts back to the candle and hold your thoughts there once again.

By doing this exercise daily, you will learn to direct your attention at will. You will learn to hold your attention in an undivided way, which is a very necessary skill to be intuitive.

90 DAY INTUITIVE PROGRAM

The 90 day program teaches a limited version of remote viewing, along with the basic mental skills of intuition. The health intuitive process I use is another means of doing an intuitive session and is taught in many of my other classes. It involves a trance state and speaking during the receptivity of the intuitive impressions.

There are three steps to the 90 day program. Step one is to develop the five mental skills required to be intuitive. You will do the five exercises throughout the program.

Step two, begins on day 31, when you will add the intuitive listening exercise. This is a meditation to develop your ability to be receptive to your intuitive voice.

Step three, starts on day 61, and adds to your intuitive perception by giving you more information and expanding your intuitive subject matter.

After day 90, continue all exercises enhancing your intuitive development.

Step 1

Developing the 5 mental skills   First 30 Days

Start by doing the exercises listed under each of the five mental skills for being intuitive. Practice all five exercises daily for 30 days. Keep a daily journal showing any improvement you notice in the areas of sensitivity, communication, focus, receptivity, and undivided attention.

Step 2

Develop intuitive listening   Add on day 31

Every morning at the same time find a quiet place to sit and do this exercise. Start by writing down a question each day of which you would truly like an answer. Then sit in a straight back chair with your feet flat on the floor, hands on your knees, and close your eyes.

Time yourself for twenty minutes. Create a state of receptivity in your mind and focus your attention in an undivided way to let the answer communicate to you clearly.

Have expectant listening. If you do not at first perceive anything, then make note of this in your journal. If any word or thought comes to your mind during this twenty minute period, write the answer in your journal. Give this some time to develop. If you are not receiving answers, ask to hear them. If you are getting answers that do not seem to apply to your questions, ask for clarity. If you feel you are making the information up, ask for intuition only to speak with you. If you do not trust the information, ask for some sign to help you know when it is a conscious thought and an intuitive impression. If you seek intuitive impressions, at some point they will begin to communicate to you.

Step 3

Develop intuitive perception   Add on day 61

You will need 30 or more 3 x 5 index cards. Have your family or friends write down places, events, people, or objects well known to you and verifiable on one side of the cards. Be sure to write only one item per card. These can be public figures and events or personal ones. They can be places you have visited or well known landmarks. They can be objects you have around the house or something famous. It doesn't matter what they are as long as you have recognition of them. These will be your intuitive targets for this exercise.

Once all cards have something written on them, shuffle them and write a four digit number on the back of each along with the type of target. There should be a different number written on one side of each card, and either a place, person, object, or event written on the other side. Do not look at the side that has the writing until the exercise is over. Only look at the side with the number.

Do this exercise each day immediately after the intuitive listening exercise.

Colors:
white, red, beige, pink, orange, blue, green, yellow, gray, amber, brown, silver, gold, black, pale, dark, shiny, dull

Sounds:
clicking, roaring, cracking, dripping, humming, muffled, rhythmic, hissing, rushing, echoes, scratching, banging, voices, quiet, loud, clanging, buzzing

Textures:
soft, hot, cold, smooth, rough, slick, sandy, sticky, prickly, hard, fluffy, coarse, lumpy, liquid, metallic, hairy, mushy, powdery, velvety, rubbery, spongy, wet

Dimensions:
oblong, diagonal, empty, heavy, below, deep, outside, massive, bulky, angular, shallow, thick, flat, square, far, broad, enclosed, open, vast, big, small, wide, pointed, narrow, long, low, high, tubular, round, tall, hollow, dense, spherical, coiled, rectangular, cylindrical, curved, inside, oval, light, edged, jagged straight

Activities:
spinning, rotating, moving, slow, fast, floating, lowering, rising, coiling, opening, closing, grasping, undulating, pulsating, hovering, gliding, still, flying

Draw one 3 x 5 index card and place it face down in front of you. Do not look at the target on the reverse side until you have completed the entire intuitive perception exercise. While still in a relaxed state from the intuitive listening exercise, say the four digit number outloud three times. Scan the lists one at a time starting with color. Write down on a piece of paper any color impressions you receive relating to the target. Then move on to the next category and do the same.

Once you have completed all five lists, begin to draw a picture of the target on a clean piece of paper. Start by using the words you gathered from the dimensions category. Once again be intuitively perceptive, and do not use any words previously gathered that do not seem correct. The drawing is another step to clarify and correct any previous information you have gathered about the target.

Continue to do this process, filling in the picture with the other descriptive words you have gathered. Be cautious to only use the words for the drawing that you feel are intuitively correct. When you have finished the intuitive perception drawing, add descriptive words like emotional response and overall atmosphere of the target to this page.

Take another clean piece of paper and write a summary about the target to complete the session. Once you are finished writing the summary, turn the index card over and look at the target.

Mark all areas you feel were correct from your drawing page and summary page. Keep your sessions and compare over the next 30 days.

EXAMPLE SESSION

If the target is the Grand Canyon it will be written on one side of a 3x5 card. On the other side will be a four digit number. Only look at the number until you have completed the session.

Page 1

This page will show the words you have written down from the list.

beige, brown, blue, dull
quiet, echoes, rushing
hot rough, hard, liquid
below, deep, outside, massive, vast, high, low
still, moving,

Page 2

Here is where the drawing is placed. Starting with the dimensional words I would draw a picture. This process is also done intuitively so you must draw what feels right from the words. It will show the contrast between something deep, low, and below, and an area high. Showing the massive, vast, outside area would also need to be drawn.

From there, I would add the other descriptive words to my drawing, showing the stillness above and the wet liquid moving slowly below. The blue of the sky and the dull, rough beige/brown of the rocks could be drawn in the picture. Words, showing where the sounds are coming from and the movements could also be helpful. You will write words on the drawing. If any word does not feel right, do not add it to the drawing.

Page 3

Here is where you write the summary. Taking both pages one and two, and adding the emotional elements you feel about the target, you write a summary.

My summary of this session might read as follows:

It felt like I was in an outside area that had something far below. It was a massive sensation, deep and far below was gentle rushing sounds. The edges were rough, brown, and hard, but it all felt very natural like I was in nature. It was still from the top but below was a sound of moving water. The upper portion was blue, and felt free, but I felt like I descended to a dark place at the bottom. Overall, it felt peaceful, but a bit overwhelming as well.

When you have completed all three pages, turn the target over and compare your answers.

Hints for better sessions:

If at any time during the intuitive perception exercise you feel you have lost focus of the target, touch the card and repeat the four digit number again.

Remember to direct your undivided attention to only the target and the intuitive impressions about the target.

Any impression, even if small, write it down on the drawing page. Communicate in writing the sensation you experience and see if the sensation builds or weakens. If it is an intuitive impression, like riding the intuitive wave, it will continue feeding you more information about the target. If it is not, it may fade.

Remember you can pick up your attention and move it gently back to the target if you feel you are drifting. Keep in mind the five mental skills you have been working with and use them to the very best of your ability during each session.

Continue to practice daily. 90 Days is only the beginning point of developing your intuition. After a year, you will notice a remarkable difference.

Do not give up even if you do not get intuitive information right away. This skill takes time. At some point you will notice a sensation, a moment of total clarity that comes through your intuition. Remember that sensation and repeat it.

PROGRESS

At the end of 90 days go back over your journal and sessions to note improvement. Even if the progress is slow, there will be hints of success and your intuition will start to communicate to you.

Keep in mind, I practiced for four years. Not the streamline process I have shown you, but I did mental and intuitive exercises for years, before my intuitive voice became strong. Patience is in order for this to develop well.

At the end of 90 days, create new targets on fresh index cards. Every 30 days, have your friends and family make 30 more cards. If you do not have others to do this for you, and you must do them yourself, it is recommended you make more, about 100 cards. The more cards the less assumptive you will be as to the target.

A variation to the written targets are pictures. Use photos from magazines and newspapers, even printing photos from the internet, can be useful resources for targets. It is also helpful if you write event, object, place, or person on the number side of the card.

Determination, consistent practice, and increasing sensitivity will get you to intuition.

REVIEW OF EXERCISES

30 Days

Do each of the five mental skill exercises daily for the duration of your program.

Take five minutes a day and describe your surroundings using only your five senses. Separate your emotional reactions from the data you receive.

Do a daily assessment of your communication skills.

Combine the sensitivity exercise with a focus exercise. While describing an object like a pencil, note how concentrated you can be on the object. Describe it in detail using all five senses, but be aware of how you are focused while doing this. When you have completed the sensory exercise, close your eyes and once again pore over all the details of the object. Keep yourself concentrating on every detail, even long after you have lost interest in the information.

Practice listening without injecting your personal thoughts or opinions. A receptive mind has no judgment or opinion, it only records what is given. Recognize the aggressive mind state by creating a sentence and writing it down. Now listen to someone else, a person in your presence, or a voice on television, and write down a sentence they have spoken. Note what is required to have a receptive state of mind.

Light a candle and place it on a table in front of you about two feet away. Place a blank piece of paper between you and the candle. While placing your undivided attention on the candle, time yourself for ten minutes. During that ten minute time frame, think of nothing other than the candle flame. If any thought or sensation, unrelated to the candle, comes into your awareness, make a check mark on the paper in front of you. If you think of something other than the candle, you have broken your attention. At that point, simply bring your thoughts back to the candle and hold your thoughts there once again.

60 Days

Start this exercise on day 31 and continue through the entire rest of the program.

Twenty minutes each day do the intuitive listening exercise.

90 Days

Start this exercise on day 61 and continue through the duration of the program.

After each intuitive listening exercise, do an intuitive perception exercise.

Journal, keeping track of your improvement.

Chapter Sixteen

ETHICS

GOLDEN RULES OF USING INTUITION

I am not a rule oriented person. I break rules just because I like to do things my way. You could even call me rebellious. I am very obedient to rules, however, when I understand their value. So as I present these rules, keep in mind they are not for strict adherence, but rather to help you understand the importance of boundaries when using this skill.

There are some basic rules one should keep in mind when using intuition. Kind thoughts are important because they reach beyond ourselves. Emotions carry more weight intuitively than thoughts. Intuition should be used to clarify perception and not to intrude. Respect free will, your own, as well as others. Play fair with intuitive negotiations. Take responsibility and stop placing your intuition outside your personal direction. Respect intuitive privacy.

KINDNESS

If your thoughts are always kind, then you have no problem with this advice. For most of us that is quite a task, however. I know of no one who keeps their thoughts always pure. From time to time, we all get upset and have unkind thoughts toward one another. This is especially true in situations where we do not even know the person involved.

There is the driver that cuts you off in traffic and the fifth telephone solicitor that calls in a single day taking you over the line. These irritating situations pop up in everyday life all the time. Even though you may believe there is no harm done from unkind thoughts, you must consider the unseen impact.

There is an indirect influence, caused upon others, through an unkind thought that is directed toward them. Intuitively, you are causing a ripple of negativity which their subconscious mind receives. They may not be consciously aware of this projection, but their autonomic system will feel it.

It is also easy to be unkind in group situations. You may disagree with someone, or there may be those you do not like. Having differing opinions may create a power struggle of thought between you and others. Your thoughts may become unkind toward them if you disagree with their principles.

In this case, negative thoughts may arise within you. You may not feel guilty because they are only thoughts. You may believe these negative thoughts have no influence as long as they are not verbalized or action taken on them. They do cause undue stress and influence on the people involved, even if it is not obvious, just as a kind thought sends an intuitive hug.

Every thought you have sends out a wave into the intuitive network that connects all of us together. Directing an unkind thought toward the driver of the car that cuts you off, the solicitor that calls at dinner time, or a board member you do not like, is sending them an intuitive slap on the face. Just because you cannot see it, does not excuse it.

In order to remain obedient to the golden rule of intuition, you must maintain kindness in your thoughts. You must be aware of all thoughts and how they may indirectly be influencing those involved. Thoughts are perceived intuitively by everyone, even when the conscious mind is unaware.

RESPONSIBILITY WITH EMOTIONS

Intuition is far easier to receive when there is a strong emotion attached. All thoughts have some emotion accompanying them. The stronger the emotion, the more influential the thought will be on an intuitive level. A thought about a person that is emotionally neutral, like an idle thought of an old friend, will not penetrate the intuition with much impact. Think of it as a weak signal. When the same thought is accompanied by a strong emotion, like wanting desperately to see the old friend, the signal strength increases, causing the impact to be much stronger.

No matter if your emotions are positive or negative, the intuitive impact is greater depending on the strength of the emotions attached. This is why monitoring our emotions is so important. You will have a loving and positive influence over others when you have strong loving emotions toward them. You will have a negative and destructive influence over others when your emotions are negative. The stronger the emotions, the stronger the signal.

Negative emotions tear down the foundation of strength and stability of people, organizations, and belief systems. Every strong negative thought will contribute to the demise of that to whom it is projected. It creates a ripple in the fabric of the subconscious mind causing some type of inner conflict to occur. It may affect people's immune systems, their feelings of self-confidence, or their ability to be decisive. It will strike the weakest area of their subconscious mind.

The golden rule of intuition asks that you monitor your emotions. Take notice if you are sending positive or negative signals. Your choice of emotions and the strength they possess, determines the type of impact you are having on the world. It is important to take emotional responsibility.

BEST USE OF INTUITION

Intuition is best used as a perception clarification tool. It can be used to gain accurate perception about a situation or a person's intent. Many misunderstandings take place because it is believed someone or some situation is for or against us. The way we see other's intent may not be accurate. In order to clarify intent and dismiss misunderstandings, use your intuition.

Remaining ignorant is not an option when you have good intuitive skills. You are able to clarify and understand the underlining motives of those involved with your life. This enables you to avoid conflict in situations, let go of harsh feelings, and create general positive attitudes.

Let your intuition guide you before jumping to conclusions. A quick response, based only on external appearances, may create an opinion that is wrong. You may slash out without justification if you have misjudged a situation. Likewise, if the misunderstanding goes the other way, you could get caught up in situations that are not good for you. Slow down your reactions and make certain your judgments are accurate by using your intuition.

RESPECT FREE WILL

Thoughts and emotions are very intertwined on an intuitive level. This causes some difficulty when trying to decipher free will. Free will is a very ambiguous thing. You must truly know who you are in order to avoid being influenced intuitively by others.

Cooperation is a valuable trait to have. We must all make compromises in order for relationships and society to function with any form of order. There is a difference, between knowingly cooperating and being coerced intuitively, to alter your free will choice.

As part of the golden rule of intuition, be aware that everyone's choices should be made freely. When you allow your intuitive projections to influence others' actions, you are failing to allow free will. Likewise, if you allow others to influence your free will, you are not recognizing your independence.

When making important decisions, do a double check with your intuition. Make certain you know yourself and your personal desires. Write them down if need be, in order to stay faithful to your personal will. By remaining faithful to your freedom to choose, you will find less resentment, frustration, and disappointment.

Respecting others' free will is just as vital. As you desire for others to behave in certain ways, remember you are influencing them intuitively. Monitor your thoughts and the strength of your emotions regarding this. Carry an attitude with you at all times of respect for individual choice. Let your thoughts and feelings be considerate and accepting.

Accepting the fact that each person owns their life and has the right to choose their life experiences will help you respect free will. Understanding the life path of others, though not the same as yours, will assist you in cooperating with this part of the intuitive golden rule.

It is so easy to project your will on others. Even when you mean well, you can be influencing the free will of someone. It is better to project concern and love, letting them make a free decision, than it is to think you know what is best for them. Thinking you know what is best is an intrusive thought in itself. You only have reign over your own life. Keep your thoughts and choices true to yourself, and respect the right for others to do the same.

At the base of this issue is control. Are others trying to control you and are you trying to control others? When your thoughts and emotions become a force pushing against another's freedom to think, feel and choose for themselves, you are trying to control them. It is something we all do but often without awareness. Compassion can only exist when free will accompanies choice.

PLAY FAIR

Intuition is just a form of communication. It is a far more direct form of communication because it is mind to mind and on a subconscious level. When you have a thought of someone, you are sending a message intuitively to them even if they are unaware. When someone has a thought about you, they are sending an intuitive message as well. Often, there is a negotiation taking place at this level long before you have any sort of physical discussion or make a decision.

Intuitive negotiations are always occurring. They can happen with or without awareness. When they are done without awareness, they often end up being selfish. Our thoughts and emotions, after all, are intended to get us what we want. You may try to intimidate, threaten or appeal to the empathy of the other person in your thoughts. Note your thinking about a situation and you will see this does happen. Your thoughts may try to negate another's position. Remember every thought and emotion has an impact, even if very small.

166

Have you ever known someone that just always seemed to get their way? I once knew a man who had the thought he deserved everything for less than it cost everyone else. He ended up getting a great deal of things for free. It wasn't because this guy was so nice, it was because he was sending a very strong signal out about wanting free things. He had little or no regard for how his desire would affect others.

Visualizing only what you want, without regard for the good of all concerned, is an unfair and unkind intuitive negotiation process. If your willfulness is causing someone to act based on your desires, then you are using your intuitive negotiations unfairly. Play fair by attaching an attitude of concern for all. It is always better to request your desire, rather than be a bully in your intuitive negotiations. Remember it is your thinking, attitudes, and emotions that make the intuitive signal what it is. If your thoughts are overbearing, then your negotiations are as well.

I once handled a real estate transaction where one party was determined to move to a location by a certain date. There was one obstacle, there was already a family living there. That didn't stop them however. They began to pray and meditate to get exactly what they wanted. Before long, hardship fell upon the family living in the home and they had to move. The other family was thrilled about getting what they wanted no matter what the cost was to the other family.

This is a prime case of unfair intuitive negotiations. An unsuspecting family had all sorts of communication directed to them regarding their move. The determined family probably had better negotiating skills and far more emotional motivation than the other family. Considering one family was unaware they were being attacked, it made the situation very unfair.

On the positive side, intuitive negotiations can be done in a fair and just way to help everyone involved. It starts by understanding what you want and that your thoughts are communicating this. I use my intuition to do what I call inner level advertising. This was great when I was in real estate. I intuitively sent out a signal inviting anyone who would benefit from the purchase of a certain property to find it. I imaged the property and the publications it could be found in. I invited interested and financially qualified parties to drive by the property and call. Our properties always sold quickly through this process.

I once used this with my two year old nephew who was in the hospital with dehydration. They needed to put an IV in his arm for fluids. Being only two, there was a great concern about his willingness to leave this in his arm. I began to negotiate intuitively with his two year old mind asking him to please leave it alone. For the next several days, he walked around the hospital pushing his IV tree and never once tried to pull it out. All I did was request his cooperation with what would help him the most.

When you desire something, start negotiating that desire intuitively long before you have a real conversation. This may sound like you are taking unfair advantage but it is not. Trust that it is only unfair when your attitude takes a selfish nature. I have trained many on how to negotiate with a spouse or loved one by this means. By setting a loving tone and requesting your desire, you are letting the information start to be digested and processed in a cooperative way. Let their needs be considered in your thoughts, and by all means, do this with respect and acceptance if it does not go your way.

If you try and manipulate or have false motives, then you are not doing this according to the golden rule of intuition. If, however, you stay true to the pureness of motives, then you have the best opportunity to intuitively negotiate wisely.

The intuitive negotiating process is no different than the external negotiating process. If you are a determined and dominate thinker, then you are probably not playing fair intuitively. Become aware of your communication style. Apply the same principles to intuitive negotiations as you do to fair external communications.

Note your emotional make up as you think of your desires. Request what you want rather than to dominate and demand. If you have a dominant attitude, then don't hide from it. Let honesty play a role here. Fine tune your skill of knowing your own motivations.

When you are honest, fair, and respectful, you will see this working more often in your favor than against you. I have used this for years and it is amazing how much more cooperative people are when you are intuitively considerate in your thoughts.

TAKE RESPONSIBILITY WITH INTUITION

Denial is like a faithful friend. This is especially true in order to remain self-centered in the way we live our lives. If we never become aware of intuition, then we never have to be responsible for it. This is really saying we never have to be responsible for the way we think and feel. The less aware we are the easier it is to be irresponsible.

We live in a competitive world. Be a winner, be number one, come out on top, are words of a self-centered society. We hear these things and pass them on with good intentions to the next generation. Do we ever stop and consider what this message is saying?

I am not promoting a society where the individual does not matter. What I am asking you to do is think about the kind of attitudes our society holds. If you do not want cut throat mentality in the world, then don't possess that mentality yourself.

A society is created by the individuals that make it up. Situations arise out of a mix of attitudes from the individuals participating. A variety of thoughts and emotions are flooding the intuitive airwaves every second. Your thoughts and emotions are in the mix. If you don't like the way things are going, then change that which you contribute.

In the broad scope of things, society is reflected in the way life plays out for the majority of people. It is reflected in the way we approach relationships and the way families are raised. It can be seen in the structure of businesses, social programs, and in the way our country treats the world. We all contribute and are influenced by our culture. We are each responsible, to some degree, for the mind set of the community, society, and country.

By taking responsibility for your personal attitudes, thoughts, emotions, and actions, you are taking responsibility for your intuitive input.

RESPECTING INTUITIVE PRIVACY

Privacy is very important to our society. No one wants someone to enter their home, look through their personal belongings, or overstep the boundaries of their personal being without permission. So why on earth do intuitives believe they have the right to go into the most personal thing of all, thoughts and feelings, without permission? For me this would be intuitive rape.

Because I teach people how to look deep into the subconscious of another person, I must address the possibilities of abuse using intuition. I must stress to each student how important respecting privacy really is.

170

It is popular among intuitives to ask the higher self for permission before doing a session. In rare cases of an emergency I have done the same. In most cases, it is very easy to just ask the individual if it is all right with them to look at their thoughts and emotions. In many cases, I have had them say no.

Once a woman was at my home and really felt her husband would benefit from a health intuitive session. I explained I couldn't do this without first asking him. She insisted it would be fine with him and could not understand my reluctancy to do the session.

I repeated my position, and even though it was inconvenient to reach him, he was working a night shift at the hospital, she called him anyway. His answer was no. He didn't want anyone in his head mulling around. It wasn't anybody else's business what he thought or felt, and he really didn't want someone looking at his internal organs. I was glad she called.

It is a moral issue of boundaries. I have been in the middle of teaching an intuitive course and inevitably I will have some student that just wants to show off. Sometimes they have good intentions and other times it is the ego that gets the best of them. Either way, they corner another student and start trying to tell them all sorts of things they see about them. This puts the student in an awkward position when they did not ask for information. They feel uncomfortable stopping the intruding student.

Being intuitive does not give us the right to be thoughtless and tactless. Losing insight into respectful courtesy doesn't impress anyone. Follow this simple rule and avoid intuitively invading another's thoughts and feelings without asking first. It doesn't take much to get permission. Simply do not use your intuition where it isn't wanted.

EPILOGUE

My journey to become intuitive took time, patience and practice. The rewards have been enormous from this effort, however. I have healed through personal crisis, seen miraculous changes in my life, and reached heights of awareness I never dreamed possible.

The intimacy I have experienced with spirit, through discovering the intuitive wave, has only increased my curiosity with the mystical side of life. There is always something around the next bend to explore and discover in the boundless world of mind and spirit. I continue to ask new questions and be guided to new frontiers within this subtle, unseen world.

As you learn to Ride The Intuitive Wave, you will discover your hidden self and the miracles awaiting your life. You are connected with this deep love and compassion I found intuitively in myself. It has been a true blessing and miracle in my life as I know it can be for others. I want to encourage you to take the first steps and become intuitive.

ABOUT THE AUTHOR

Linda Eastburn, a nationally acclaimed intuitive, has helped thousands of people develop their intuitive potential. She is a featured guest on radio and television programs throughout the world and has lectured at numerous universities and conferences. Her radio and television program, Anomalies, was broadcast to a worldwide audience.

Her pioneering techniques, presented in an understandable and compassionate manner, are indispensable and inspiring to anyone desiring the manifestation of miracles in their life. The results, she witnessed in herself and others, utilizing easily learned techniques, inspired her to be the founder of the International Academy of Intuitive Arts.

Suggested Reading

Aldana, Jacquelyn, *The 15-Minute Miracle Revealed*. Los Gatos, CA, Inner Wisdom Publications, 1995

Condron, Barbara, *Kundalini Rising: Mastering Creative Energies*. Missouri, SOM, 1992

Condron, Daniel, *Permanent Healing*. Missouri, SOM, 1992

Dossey, Larry, *Healing Words: Power of Prayer and the Practice of Medicine*. San Francisco: Harper, 1993

Goleman, Daniel, *Working With Emotional Intelligence*. New York: Bantam Books, 1998

Hay, Louis, *You Can Heal Your Life*. Carlsbad, California, Hay House, 1987

Keeney, Bradford, *The Energy Break: Recharge Your Life With Autokinetics*. New York: Golden Books, 1998

Pert, Candace, *Molecules of Emotions: Why You Feel The Way You Feel*. New York, Scribner, 1997

Reid, Daniel, *The Complete Book of Chinese Health and Healing*. New York, Barnes & Noble 1998

Schultz, Ron, *Unconventional Wisdom: Twelve Remarkable Innovators Tell How Intuition Can Revolutionize Decision Making*. New York, HarperCollins, 1994

Smith, Thompson, Angela, *Remote Perceptions: Out-of-Body Experiences, Remote Viewing, and Other Normal Abilities*. Charlottesville, VA, Hampton Roads, 1998

Talbot, Michael, *The Holographic Universe*. New York, HarperPerennial, 1992

Wise, Anna, *The High Performance Mind*. New York: Tarcher/Putman, 1997

Private Intuitive Sessions

By phone or in person.
Credit cards accepted
CALL   417-863-1377

Linda is available for speaking engagements, workshops, and personal sessions.

Manifestation Tutorial

Linda offers a personal two day life changing tutorial for those wanting to experience rapid progress. The tutorial includes a complete whole life intuitive assessment, life coaching sessions, and an orientation to new patterns of living.

Don't settle for a life less than what you deserve. Learn to live from a state of intuitive love. Let your relationships, prosperity, and life purpose come to you with ease. See where you have come from, where you are now, and learn to create the future you want. Your life is waiting to be blessed.

Internationally Academy of Intuitive Arts

Distance Courses

Health Intuitive Course

Remote Viewing Course

Hypnosis Course

Intuitive Development Course

Manifestation Course

Call for a free brochure about the courses
417-863-1377

Linda Eastburn, PO Box 3194
Springfield, MO 65808